About the Author

Margaret Molloy works for Mayo Library Service in Ballina library and lives in Bohola, Co. Mayo. Her work has been published in national and local magazines and newspapers, including *Ireland's Own*, *Ireland's Eye*, *The Irish Catholic*, *The Western People*, *The Mayo News* and *The Connaught Telegraph*. She was involved in the publication of *Bohola: Its History and its People* (1992) and *The Martin Sheridan Story* (1998), and was co-author with Professor Peter Reid, Robert Gordon University, Aberdeen, of 'Church and State: Censorship and Political Interference in the Libraries of County Mayo' in *The Journal of Library and Information History* in May 2013. Margaret holds a BA in English and History and an MSc in Library and Information Studies.

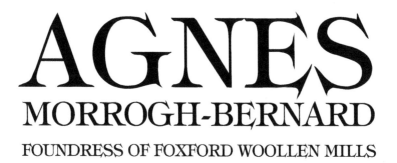

AGNES
MORROGH-BERNARD
FOUNDRESS OF FOXFORD WOOLLEN MILLS

MARGARET MOLLOY

FOREWORD BY MARY ROBINSON

MERCIER PRESS

MERCIER PRESS
Cork
www.mercierpress.ie

© Margaret Molloy, 2014
© Foreword: Mary Robinson, 2014

ISBN: 978 1 78117 330 5

A CIP record for this title is available from the British Library

Table of Contents

Abbreviations

BMD	Births Marriages and Deaths
CDB	Congested Districts Board
DATI	Department of Agriculture and Technical Instruction
IAOS	Irish Agricultural Organisation Society
JDHS	*Journal of the Donegal Historical Society*
JWHS	*Journal of the Westport Historical Society*
MMM	Medical Missionaries of Mary
RSCG	Religious Sisters of Charity Generalate Archives, Sandymount, Dublin

Acknowledgements

～∞～

MY SINCERE THANKS to Mary Robinson; I am deeply indebted to her for writing the foreword to this book.

My gratitude and thanks to Sister Marie Bernadette O'Leary, Archivist, Sisters of Charity, Sandymount, Dublin for all her help while I was researching material for this book. Also Sister Monica Byrne, who typed a copious amount of material. Gerry Devaney, Local History Archivist, Linenhall Library, Belfast; Christine Finlay, Librarian, Omagh Library, County Tyrone; Collette O'Flaherty, Archivist, and James Harte of the Manuscripts Department in the National Library of Ireland; Dr Raymond Refausse, Archivist, Representative Church Body Library, Churchtown, County Dublin; also Robert Gallagher and Mary Furlong, Assistant Librarians; Noella Dowling, Archivist, Dublin Diocesan Archives, Drumcondra, Dublin; Michael Keane, Archivist, Military Archives, Rathmines, Dublin; Evelyn Roche, Archivist, Guinness Archive, St James's Gate, Dublin; Gillian Kirby, Reader Advisor, British Archives, Kew Gardens, Richmond; Laura Hobbs, Assistant Archivist, Windsor Palace; Sally Goodsir, Assistant Curator of Decorative Arts, St James's Palace, London; Wendy Hawke, Archivist, London Metropolitan Archives; Juline Baird, Assistant Archivist, Scottish Borders Council, Heritage Hub, Hawick, Scotland; Cathy Hobkirk, Local History Archives Centre, Hawick, Scotland; Lord Aberdeen, Mains of Haddo, Tarves, Ellon, Aberdeenshire; also Marge Jones and Moira Minty; Eileen Morrison, Cheltenham; Lisa Wood, Cheltenham; and Jan at Cheltenham Library.

Fr Aiden Keenan and Teresa Johnston, St Matthew's Parish, Bally-macarret, Belfast; Michael Lynch, Local History Department, Tralee County Library, Kerry; Mary Conefrey, Local History Department, Ballinamore County Library, Leitrim; Sister Pat Casey, Pastoral Assistant, Ballaghaderreen, County Roscommon; Austin Vaughan, Mayo County Librarian; Mary Gannon, Senior Executive Librarian, Castlebar; Sinéad McCoole, Curator, Jackie Clarke Library, Ballina, for her help and advice; Ivor Hamrock, Local History Department, Mayo County Library, Castlebar; James Laffey, Editor, *Western People*, Ballina; Ailish Irvine, Irvine Training, Kiltimagh, County Mayo; Ivars Zauers, Ballina; Peter Hynes, Manager, Mayo County Council; Frankie Devaney, Foxford; Margaret Maloney, Stonehall, Foxford; Emma Sherry, Foxford; Michael Stanton, Foxford; Joe Queenan, Manager, Foxford Woollen Mills for his donation; Imelda Turnbull, Foxford and Galway; Eithne Brogan, Foxford; Ben Kimmerling, Pontoon; Canon Michael Joyce PP, Bohola; Brendan Walsh, Researcher, Mayo North Heritage Centre; Michael Feeney Castlebar; Susannah Russell, Mallow Heritage Centre, Cork; Elaine Harrington, Special Collections Librarian, UCC, Cork. A very special word of thanks to Lieutenant Larry Scallan, Stephens Barracks, Kilkenny, for all his help.

A special word of thanks also to Adrian Bourke, Solicitor, Ballina, for providing family photographs and information on the family link with the Morrogh family. To Michelle Garrett of Adrian P. Bourke & Co., for all her help. To Jackie Kelly, Bohola, for her invaluable help with the technical side of the project. To my colleagues in Ballina Library; Barbara and Majella Varley, Siobhan King, Angela Keegan, Deirdre Butler and Paula Ryan. Thank you for your encouragement and support.

To Caroline, Shirley, Eva, Fintan and Francis, thank you for your help and support. To my dear Frank, who would have been so proud to have seen this book published. Thank you.

Foreword
by Mary Robinson

∽

I AM HAPPY to contribute to this book because Agnes Morrogh-Bernard, or Mother Mary Arsenius as she was called, was a heroine of my childhood. On visits from Ballina with my mother to buy blankets and dressing gowns from the Foxford Mills, I heard of how she had come to Foxford in 1891 as a Sister of Charity and had been overwhelmed by the poverty in the area. The story of how she had been helped by a 'black Northern Presbyterian' to set up the looms which began the mill was inspiring. I learned that Mother Arsenius was related to my father's mother, Eleanor Bourke (née MacCaulay). A cousin of hers, Jane Morrogh, married William Orme Paget Bourke, my father's grandfather, and she baptised all her seven children Catholic, initially without the knowledge of her husband, who was a Protestant.

I made my first visit to the Foxford Mills as President of Ireland in April 1991 to turn the sod for the planned visitor centre there. It was my first official visit to Mayo as President and there was a huge turnout. I was invited to sound the mill hooter to start the second century of what is known as the Foxford Story. John Charles Lawson, the grandson of John Charles Smith, of Caledon, County Tyrone – the man who helped Mother Agnes Morrogh-Bernard establish her industry – was present at the ceremony that day and was afforded a special place of honour. My father accompanied me. For the first time he spoke of a childhood memory of being brought to Foxford as a five-year-old to meet Mother Arsenius. He confessed that he was terrified by her as she was dressed in black with a big hooded veil that brushed against him when she tried to kiss him.

During a second visit as President in 1992 I was pleased to see Noel Dorr, who introduced me to his mother. She had nursed Mother Arsenius during the months prior to her death in Foxford in 1932. She was from Limerick, and told me that it was when she came to Foxford for that nursing position that she met her future husband, a designer at the Foxford Mills.

It seemed fitting, somehow, that the early planning meetings to discuss the establishment of the Mary Robinson Centre in Ballina, between representatives of Mayo County Council, NUIG, local Ballina business representatives, my brother Adrian, and Nick and myself, would take place in the coffee shop of the Foxford Mills, where we would pass by a framed photograph of my early heroine, Mother Arsenius, Agnes Morrogh-Bernard. I commend Ballina librarian Margaret Molloy for telling her story and ensuring she can be a heroine for a whole new generation.

Early Years

AGNES MORROGH-BERNARD was born in Cheltenham, Gloucestershire, England, on 24 February 1842. Her father, John Morrogh, came from a prominent Catholic family in Glanmire, County Cork. On inheriting the Bernard estates in Kerry from his maternal grandmother, he became known as John Morrogh-Bernard. While attending school in Bath, in England, he met Agnes's mother, Frances Mary Blount, who was staying with her grandmother. The Blounts were an old English Catholic family. The couple married in Cheltenham in 1841 and later returned

CERTIFIED COPY of an ENTRY
Pursuant to the Births and Deaths Registration Act 1953

FE 332358

The birth certificate of Agnes Morrogh-Bernard.

to Ireland, first settling in Cork and later at Sheheree House in Kerry in 1849. A notice of their marriage appeared in *The Freeman's Journal:*

> On the 18th instant at the Catholic Chapel, Cheltenham, John Morrogh-Bernard Esq., second son of Edward Morrogh Esq., of Glanmire House, Co. Cork to Frances Mary, only child of Joseph Blount Esq., of Hurstbourne Tarrant, Hampshire.[1]

This area of Kerry had been ravaged by the potato famine of the previous years, and hunger and poverty had claimed many victims. A young Agnes, although cushioned by wealth, was not blind to the terrible conditions that prevailed among the poor. *The Kerryman* reported that:

> The daughter of an Irish landed aristocrat might have been pardoned if she had closed her eyes to the poverty and misery of the Kerry countryside after the famine years. Instead the sight of a poor woman, begging in the kitchen of Sheheree House to be allowed to eat the boiled nettles that were intended for the poultry, set her on a path that led her to the doors of the Sisters of Charity Novitiate and ultimately to a unique place among the greatest women not only of Ireland but of the world – in a most unworldly sense.[2]

Agnes, as a young girl, had witnessed a starving woman eating a mash prepared for the turkeys at the back door of their house, and it seems it was something she never forgot. Her work among the poverty-stricken people of the West in later years would support this.

A stubbornness inherent in Agnes's character at a very young age is evident from the following account:

I remember when I was about four, my mother had begun to teach me little lessons. She asked me to spell 'who'. I was particularly self-willed that day. I stood before her, with my hands behind my back and refused. My mother pointed to a birch twig tied with blue ribbons, which hung in the nursery, and which was known as Betty Birch. All to no avail. I stamped my little feet, and kept saying, 'me won't spell "who", me won't.'[3]

Betty Birch was used unsparingly on Agnes. It was not the only form of punishment. One day she was sent in deep disgrace to the nursery without dinner. To mortify her pride and bend her stubborn will, the butler was ordered to bring her a crust of dry bread and a glass of water on a silver tray. The humiliation was fruitless. Peace was restored and pardon given only when a visitor intervened and carried her down on his shoulder.[4] The stubbornness that Agnes displayed would serve her well in later years, when many trials and problems were to be placed on her young shoulders.

Agnes may well have inherited the trait of generosity and kindness from her forebears as is evident in the following report:

The altar of St Joseph's chapel, erected at the expense of Mr. Morrogh-Bernard, is one of the gems of the Cathedral. The font (exclusively carved in Caen stone) represents the Nativity of our Lord. The plinth of red Fermoy marble, the pillars of Galway marble resting on pillars of purest Carrara with beautiful curved capitals of Caen stone. The slab is of Sicilian marble. The whole is highly creditable to the taste of the gentleman by whom it has been erected and to the skill of the artists employed by Messrs Farmer of Westminster, the contractors.[5]

Agnes had a very privileged life, and she was adored by her

father. She attended the prestigious Laurel Hill convent school in Limerick, founded by Victoire d'Houet, who had established the order of the Faithful Companions of Jesus (FCJ) at Amiens in France in 1820. *The Kerryman* reported:

> While at Laurel Hill, Agnes formed the habit of going down to pray in the chapel at night when the others were asleep, but was discovered and her midnight vigils forbidden.[6]

Her education was rounded off with two years at a finishing school in Paris. On her return to the family home in 1860, her parents assumed she would settle into the accepted lifestyle of her class, one of ease and gentility, and the eventual wealthy marriage. Agnes was not short of male admirers, and her engagement was announced unofficially to a baronet, but a stronger force was pulling at her heartstrings. She visited the Irish Sisters of Charity convent in Cork with her aunt and shortly afterwards began her novitiate with the Order at Harold's Cross, Dublin, in 1863. She was professed in 1866 and took the name Arsenius. Her father was distraught when Agnes entered the order.

She herself said of the day that she parted from him to enter the convent that 'nothing ever

Agnes on her profession in 1866.

again would pierce her, so great was the sorrow they both had endured'.[7]

Agnes's decision to enter the Order showed a determination to actively serve the poor.[8] She later recalled the day of her profession:

> It was five and a half years after the death of our reverend Foundress, Mary Aikenhead, that I received the habit on 12 January 1866 from the late Cardinal Cullen, who told us that we were to be ready to spend our lives among the Blacks. It was the only time he was ever known to preach at a reception or profession and I have never forgotten it, always having a hankering for the Foreign Missions.[9]

Later in her life, Agnes was given the opportunity to campaign for religious Sisters to serve in the foreign missions, as in the case of Mary Charles Walker. To a certain degree, her hankering for the foreign missions was appeased if not wholly fulfilled.

Mary Aikenhead.

The Sisters of Charity were founded in 1815 by Cork-born Mary Aikenhead, daughter of Dr David Aikenhead, a wealthy apothecary and property owner of Scottish descent, and Mary Stackpole, an aristocratic Catholic from a wealthy merchant family. Their motto became *Caritas Christi Urget Nos* (the love of Christ urges us). The constitution of the congregation called for vows of chastity, poverty and obedience, as well as a fourth vow obliging the Sisters to devote their lives to the service of the poor. The Order based their non-specific approach of perpetual service to the poor on that of the French Daughters of Charity.[10]

The Sisters of Charity opened their first convent, on North William Street in Dublin, in September 1815. At the centenary celebration in 1915, Bishop Donnelly, of Chania in Crete, preached the sermon. He told the congregation present that:

> The Sisters began by taking care of orphans, the most helpless, as the most innocent of God's poor … Soon North William St became too small, and a refuge for young girls in training for domestic service was secured in Stanhope St, … then it was Cork and then Gardiner St, followed by Sandymount, where the terrible scourge of the cholera in 1832 opened up a new field of labour in nursing the afflicted patients … I may, perhaps, be permitted to single out a few of the foundations that deserve special mention, because of the enterprise they connote – such as the care of the poor penitents, as in Donnybrook; the care and education of the blind, as in Merrion; the care – and what shall I call it – the salvation of the dying, as in the Hospice; and the Convent of Divine Providence in Foxford, where an unpretentious industrial work, started to give badly needed employment, developed into the fine technical schools and woollen mills, which keep constantly employed individuals,

and provide an easily accessible market for the wool of the surrounding cottiers.[11]

The Sisters played a pivotal part in the health and welfare of the poor of Dublin:

> The Sisters established the first Catholic hospital, St Vincent's, in Dublin, in 1834. They were the first active religious congregation formed in Ireland.[12]

In contrast to secular hospitals, St Vincent's provided help not only for the body but also for the soul:

> Many, who were refused entrance to the hospital by the doctors, because their illnesses were not deemed serious enough or because they were terminally ill, were nevertheless admitted by the sister in charge for her own set of reasons.[13]

Agnes's first assignment after being professed as an Irish Sister of Charity was as a teacher in Dublin's Gardiner Street, where she taught ragged and miserably poor children. She was then appointed as headmistress of the King's Inns Street School, where she had charge of 1,200 pupils.

> For a decade she laboured faithfully in the national school, at King's Inns Street. Poor health forced her temporarily to abandon her work in 1869; afterwards she served at the Orphanage at Mountjoy Street, the Magdalen Asylum at Donnybrook, and the Orphanage at Lakelands, in Sandymount in Dublin.[14]

In 1876 Agnes was sent westward to Ballaghaderreen, County

Roscommon, to become rectress of the convent. One of the nuns there was a member of the Ousley-Higgins family of Galway, and her share in the estate was the property of the order. The survival of the Ballaghaderreen convent relied on rents from the Ousley-Higgins tenants in Galway, and during the Land War rents were not forthcoming. The Mother General in Dublin wanted the nuns to leave, but Agnes insisted they stay.

> For fourteen years she and her Sisters toiled in the area of poverty, education, and social improvement in the town and the surrounding area. Agnes was so concerned about the hungry schoolchildren that she provided a stirabout (porridge) breakfast for about seventy to one hundred children. Donations were sent from England, America and even as far away as Australia and all of these helped to pay for the meals.[15]

Agnes set up a dispensary near the entrance to the convent. It was called St Martin's. There, people were treated and looked after in their hundreds. An industrial school was also established, and the government gave a grant for a school of seventy-five girls in Ballaghaderreen.[16]

> The Sisters acquired a laundry tender for church vestments and the convent also incorporated a national school and dormitories which enabled the nuns to get industrial school status in 1886 for seventy-five girls.[17]

Agnes also established a bakery, a pharmacy and a lending library. In her notes she recorded the following:

> Mary and Kate Conroy arrived in the convent. Their family had a spinning wheel and a loom which were given to the convent.

The loom had once belonged to Mr. Fox, from the Technical School in Manchester, who came to give instructions on the use of a loom sent from Bradford. It was an up-to-date model and cost £10. Towels and homespuns were then made up by the girls in the Industrial School. They were also trained in needlework, and dressmaking, lace-making, crochet, knitting and button making.[18]

Agnes used every means to push the sale of these goods, even canvassing for orders through the post, and personally visiting shopkeepers.

Agnes was lucky, in that Dr Francis McCormack was the Bishop of Achonry at this time and he was known for his kindness to the poor, with crowds of them flocking daily to his door. In him, Agnes had a staunch ally in her fight for the betterment of conditions for these poverty-stricken people.

Agnes celebrated the silver jubilee of her religious profession in Ballaghaderreen on 16 January 1891. Eighty years after Agnes left the town, the Sisters of Charity decided to withdraw their Sisters from the convent there. In 1971 the Sisters of Mercy bought the convent for £30,000 and took up residence. The departure of the Sisters of Charity was recalled by Sister Regina Lydon, a Sister of Mercy:

> It was both a sad and emotional day for them. One Sister spent thirty-four years in Ballaghaderreen. They had left their dead behind them in the little convent cemetery at the back of the convent. The Sisters of Mercy had Mass offered for them on the day of their exodus. A half day was given in the school to mark their going away. Two cars arrived to take them back to Dublin. It was the end of an era for them. They had given a long and dedicated service to the people of Ballaghaderreen.[19]

It was in Ballaghaderreen that Agnes first encountered Anne Deane, who would become a lifelong friend and benefactress. Anne was an aunt of John Dillon, who was MP for East Mayo at Westminster at this time. She had been married to Edward Deane, a struggling solicitor, and had lived in Foxford, County Mayo, for a short time. Her husband died at a young age and she returned to Ballaghaderreen, where she inherited the family business, known as Monica Duff's. It was a thriving business that catered to every need in the community. Maurice Manning gives the following description:

> Anne Deane was a woman of character, organisational skills, and good business instincts ... she was acquainted with most of the leading political and ecclesiastical figures of the time. President of the Ladies Land League in 1891, she was noted for her charity and benevolence and she had strong nationalist views on most of the major issues of those years.[20]

Anne Deane had lived in Foxford and had seen at first hand the terrible poverty crippling the people. She begged Agnes to establish a convent there to try to help the community. She entreated Mrs Margison, the Mother General of the Sisters of Charity in Dublin, with the same request.[21] Mrs Margison agreed, promising to lend £1,000, on which Anne Deane promised to pay the interest for five years. Bishop Lyster wrote to the Protestant police sergeant in Foxford asking him if there was any house available in the district 'suitable for a lady with small means and a family of ten or twelve'. Subsequently, a house and land valued at £475 was purchased. Agnes and Sisters Wall, Smollen, Meyler and Doran arrived in Foxford on 25 April 1891. The sight that met their eyes was not for the faint-hearted. *The Daily Chronicle* carried a description of Foxford in 1897:

The country is dreary, the earth dark, sodden with rain as if it never had time to dry between one shower and another, and covered with boulders that offer an almost insurmountable obstacle to cultivation. The resident gentry are few and apparently indifferent for the most part to the condition of the people so long as rents are paid. To pay these rents the men usually migrate to England for the summer and autumn, and find work with farmers, leaving their wives and children to garner as best they may their miserable harvest. When the month of November sets in a period of winter idleness, no labour to do, and no market for it if done.[22]

The convent was opened and blessed by Bishop Lyster on 26 April 1891, and the management of the national schools was given to the Sisters, who found the roll call was small indeed in proportion to the population. Marguerite Moore describes the efforts of the nuns in promoting national-school education among poor children:

A disused corn store near the convent was changed into a large airy schoolhouse which could accommodate three times the number of children on the lists. When the nuns sought to gather in pupils they found that want of clothing was an obstacle to attendance. The kindness of friends helped them to surmount this difficulty. A warm breakfast of mush and milk was given the younger children after their walk.[23]

Agnes knew that living conditions in the areas surrounding the town were indeed horrendous and that they must be improved. She understood the poverty and deprivation of the people. The animals that were housed inside the cabins were there because of necessity. The cows gave off warmth, and the pig paid the rent

The old corn store by the River Moy.

to the landlord, which was essential for the family to remain on the property. Whatever their comments, most visitors eventually understood the pig's basic function for the peasant family; in the often repeated phrase, it was 'the gintleman that pays the rint'.[24] In her memoirs Agnes recorded the following:

> Our Missioners visited the various townlands and many little villages, some of very few scattered cabins and others more pretentious, of perhaps a dozen houses or so. To reach these the Sisters had to leave the road and cross fields and almost always had to pick their way as best they could past very unpleasant manure heaps, lucky if they found a stone or two to step on; often there was the narrowest little causeway between two of these abominations. If your foot slipped – tragedy! The doors of the cabins opened on to these. We decided in the face of all discouragement, that we would wage war against these unhealthy manure pits. For a moment we did not condemn the people for the sordidness of their surroundings – the blame lay elsewhere. For long generations no one had taken any interest in the lives or well-being of these poor souls.[25]

Many travel writers visited the West of Ireland and described what they found there. One of these writers, Thomas Reid, described a manure pit on a visit in 1822:

> Almost every cabin is decorated with a pit before the door for the reception of the sweepings of the house, and every sort of filth, which, from the rains, and the foul water of washing and other domestic uses, is generally in a half-fluid state throughout the winter, and emits an intolerable exhalation in the summer.[26]

In March 1913, in the journal *Studies*, Conor Maguire, the district medical officer for Claremorris, County Mayo, stated:

> If the diseases of poverty were to be eradicated in urban and rural Ireland then the first priority had to be improved housing.[27]

Besides cholera and typhus, which were recognised as being synonymous with starvation and poverty, a disease also rampant at this time was tuberculosis, or TB as it was commonly known. It affected the lungs initially and often wiped out whole families.

Agnes and her Sisters did not need anyone to tell them that housing had to be improved. They knew that if nothing was done, disease would continue to fell the people before it. So they set about improving the habitats of the poor, by whitewashing, and having chimneys and windows fitted. Separate buildings were constructed for animals, either as adjuncts to houses, or on the holding. The dreaded 'manure pit' was removed from near the dwelling. A group who had attended the Connaught Exhibition in 1895 described what they encountered. *The Weekly Irish Times* carried the following report:

In our four day's march we visited close on two hundred habitations, chiefly of the poorest class. We found, in many instances that the manure pit, which for generations had held its place at the door steps had been removed and the cesspool of ages cleaned out, drained and converted into a garden and gravelled approach to the door. We found whitewashed walls and new windows or chimneys and roof, where never were such things before, the door being often the only exit for smoke or inlet for light into a single chamber domiciling eight or ten human beings with what animals they might possess. We saw vegetables and flowers grown and flower beds tastefully arranged and tended where vegetables and flowers never grew before and by children who never saw a flower garden. We saw that in most instances the misplaced matter hitherto surrounding the cottages in a sea of filth had been relegated to a place where it might be no longer called dirt, but a valuable adjunct to the farm. We found that a separate apartment had been provided for the pig, who no longer sleeps with the family.[28]

These improvements did not go unnoticed. In 1895 the local magistrate, Mr Standish O'Grady-McDermott, stated:

It is no exaggeration to say that all the Acts of Parliament ever passed have not effected in those remote rural districts as much in the cause of sanitation and health, as had been done in a few months by the example and gentle influence of the Sisters of Charity.[29]

Beside the convent itself a small dispensary was built, where medicine and other charity was distributed to the needy. In this area, Mayo was probably the worst equipped county in Ireland, with O'Grada noting that in 1841 there was only one medical practitioner for every six thousand people.[30] At this time Dr

Ferran was the practising GP in Foxford and he had to cover a huge area. Agnes wrote to friends, relatives and anybody who might be willing to donate items of clothing or anything that could improve the lives of the poor.

Spiritually, the Sisters effected profound change also:

> When the Sisters went to Foxford, morale among the people and the priests was low. The parish church was badly maintained. There was no weekday Mass; for the first two years of the Sisters' time in the town there was no homily given on Sunday. After two years' persuasion by Mother Arsenius the parish priest eventually gave a homily on Good Friday.[31]

One of the Sisters' first tasks was the undertaking of catechism lessons for the children in their makeshift schools. For the adults they established sodalities, taking charge of these in the neighbouring parishes as well. The Sisters were responsible for starting the First Friday devotions and Corpus Christi processions in the parish.

> The first ever retreat for workers in Ireland was conducted in Foxford during Easter of 1913. The Pioneer total Abstinence Association was introduced in 1914. In 1915, Agnes observed the 'Quarant Ore', a forty-hour devotion period to the Blessed Sacrament, which was the first time this particular devotion took place in the Diocese of Achonry. What began in Foxford soon became a model for other parishes to imitate.[32]

In 1862 the Sisters of Charity had established a convent, in Benada, County Sligo, a few miles from Foxford.

This property had been the ancestral home of the Jones family, and in 1858 one of the last official acts of Mary Aikenhead was the signing of a document accepting the property of Benada, consisting of a manor and about 900 acres of land and the rents that went with it.[33]

A tough task lay ahead of the Sisters when they arrived in Benada. Mary Peckham Magray gives the following account of their arrival in the place:

> They found the neighbourhood in a state of neglect of every Christian duty. They attended the parish chapel and saw that few adults and no children came to church, and only two or three persons approached for Holy Communion on the first Sunday of the month. After just two years of work, the Sisters reported that men, women and children, who had previously appeared indifferent about performing the essential duties of their religion, now crowded into the convent school for instruction.[34]

The Sisters had a refining influence in Benada:

> The profane ballads and songs of a questionable nature hitherto popular in the locality, gradually faded away after the arrival of these Sisters to be replaced by the hymns and sacred songs taught by the Sisters.[35]

Benada convent became a direct casualty of the famine conditions prevailing in the winter of 1879. The Sisters' only means of support were the rents paid by the Jones' tenants, which had been donated to them with the property by the family. They had no alternative but to pack up and leave and return to Dublin. The convent closed in February 1880. In order to return to

Benada they had to find a source of income that would leave them independent of the rents and so they decided to establish a grant-endowed industrial school. The Sisters returned on 15 August 1881. The foundation stone of the industrial school was laid by Bishop MacCormack.

In both Foxford and Benada it was apparent that the nuns effected quite a change in both the secular and spiritual areas to the betterment of the community. However, for Agnes and her Sisters those innovations were minor. The changes to farming practice would not suffice for the people to earn a living, as the holdings were too small and too congested. If conditions were to improve for the people of the district, something on a far bigger scale would have to be implemented. Agnes would need to have providence on her side.

Foxford

FOXFORD'S HISTORY IS associated with the Bingham family who were ancestors of the Earl of Lucan. In 1678 Henry Bingham obtained (by cheating, local account runs) the lands and the castle of John Burke of Bellanaloob. He left the castle and built a mansion, which he called Newbrook, and this became the family seat in the parish of Robeen, near Claremorris, in County Mayo. The house was destroyed by fire in 1837.

> In 1800, John Bingham M.P. was created Baron of Newbrook, given the title Lord Clanmorris. It is recorded that Lord Clanmorris in addition to being granted a peerage, got £23,000 for his vote for the Act of Union.[1]

In 1801 Bingham was granted a charter to build a new town, which was Foxford. The charter was also in recognition of his support for the Act of Union. To secure his town charter, Bingham promised to fund and build an infantry barracks.

> His offer, coming so soon after the dramatic events of 1798, must have been music to the ears of Dublin Castle. Foxford was now regarded as a key bridgehead between the two principal towns in Co. Mayo – Castlebar and Ballina.[2]

When Agnes and her Sisters founded the convent in Foxford, a lot of the land was owned by John George Barry Bingham, DL, JP, the 5th Baron Clanmorris. He married Matilda Catherine Ward, heiress to Bangor Castle, County Down, where he resided. He served as aide-de-camp to the Lord Lieutenant of Ireland between 1876 and 1878, as Deputy Lieutenant of County Mayo and as a Justice of the Peace for County Down and County Galway. He died in 1916 and was succeeded by his son Arthur, 6th Baron Clanmorris.[3] An account of the lands and tenantry of the 5th Baron Clanmorris is given by Finlay Dun:

> From Manulla Junction to Foxford and thence to Swineford [*sic*], are thousands of acres of poor red bog, much of it flat and difficult to drain, sparsely scattered villages of mud hovels, numerous smallholders on rundale or rudely-striped farms, cultivation done expensively and untidily by the spade, no attempt at autumn clearing or upturning of the soil to the ameliorating influences of frost, thrashing of light indifferently saved oats effected by the flail, and winnowing in pristine form, conducted outside the barn with the assistance of the western breezes. Lord Clanmorris and Mrs Rushley are the chief owners of these poor subjects about Foxford ... [T]he parish of Killbelfad, in the Union of Ballina, near Foxford, belonging to Lord Clanmorris, extends to 475 acres and is let to thirty-nine tenants. The total land valuation is 70*l.*, the tenement valuation is only 15*l.*, which does not say much for the condition and accommodation of the thirty-nine dwelling houses ... On the townland of Cuinbeg, measuring 337 acres, Lord Clanmorris has seventeen tenants; the total valuation of the land is 25*l.* 10*s;* the tenement valuation is 8*s*–15*s*; the rental is about 20 per cent over the valuation. These tenants have land enough, but it is woefully poor, like much else in this neighbourhood, it is not made the best of. The Bellass townland, in the Strachean electoral division, is divided among forty-two tenants, whose

tenement valuation is only 7*l*. 15*s;* their land is valued for Poor Law purposes at 112*l*. 5*s;* many are paying less than 40*s*. of annual rent. It is a most puzzling problem how these poor people on indifferent land can be improved. It is not the rent that pauperises them; it is the want of judiciously applied systematic industry.[4]

To understand conditions in the West it is necessary to go back to the 'Plantation' of Connaught, when:

> Irish occupiers of land were disposed of. Their fertile holdings given to the planters, and they themselves driven to the moors and bogs of Donegal, Mayo, Galway, Kerry and West Cork. They were now tenants-at-will to landlords, who had also been dispossessed of their estates in eastern fertile regions, or to new British landlords who had been granted estates in the West.[5]

W. L. Micks, secretary of the Congested Districts Board (CDB), summed up the reason for the conditions that prevailed in the West of Ireland:

> With very few exceptions tenants were regarded only as occupiers from whom the highest possible rents should be extracted. There was little, if any, care for their welfare or comfort. Holdings were given to the bidders of the highest rents, occupants being evicted if they did not agree to pay, and pay such rents as were demanded or offered. If a tenant made any improvements beyond the construction of a cottage or hovel, or if he appeared to live in any state of comfort beyond the low average of the district, it was assumed that he could pay a higher rent, and the rent was accordingly raised. It is no wonder that in such circumstances tenants should continue

to live in squalor, rags and discomfort, and this condition was assumed to be the natural and inevitable state of the tenantry by those who visited them, and even by the tenants themselves. The increase in population in the West prior to the Great Famine of 1845–48 was partly due to the encouragement of landlords of numerous holdings on their estates, so that the number of voters on the Parliamentary register might be increased under legislation passed in the last decade of the eighteenth century. The political influence of a landlord largely depended upon the number of votes he could control, because tenants were obliged to vote as directed by their landlord or else be prepared to receive a notice to quit. The sub-division of holdings or the creation of new smallholdings was accordingly allowed by landlords, even when it must have been known that few tenants could make only a bare subsistence, while on a failure of the crop, public relief was the only alternative to starvation.[6]

Foxford was one of the poorest regions in the county. The reason for it being so impoverished is explained by Crowley *et al.*:

> Firstly, the potato famine of 1845–1847 decimated the country-side. The people of Connaught suffered most grievously during the Famine. According to the 1841 and 1851 Censuses Connaught's population declined from 1.4 to 1.0 million in that decade. In 1841, almost four-fifths of the families were employed in agriculture on very small farms, the average being less than ten acres. Connaught was the least industrialised and least commercialised province in the country.[7]

Historians impute various factors to be the cause of the Famine:

> The sub-division of land, which was aggravated by the system

of joint tenancy known as 'rundale'. Land held in rundale was rented in common and divided up, so that each tenant received a portion of the land, good, bad and medium. Rundale combined with sub-division provided the merest fragments of land.[8]

Over-reliance on the potato was another factor which contributed to the Famine. The potato was the staple food of the people at this time and it was very easy to grow in the poor land of Connaught. Potato growing did not require much maintenance, thus the crop became the mainstay of the family. However, Joel Mokyr states that the cause of the Famine was far more complex, and was contingent on many factors and not just one specific cause:

> Conflicts, poorly defined property rights, bargaining and transaction costs, inflexible contracts, imperfect information flows and a variety of similar phenomena which economists regard as imperfections and failures of the market mechanism to allocate resources and to permit and generate economic growth.[9]

Ciara Breathnach claims that:

> Subdivision and subsequent over-dependence on smallholdings was considered a primary cause of the 1847 famine and the consolidation of farms was perceived as the best method of preventing a recurrence.[10]

There are many differing opinions on the cause of the poverty in the West that exacerbated the effects of the Famine. Christine Kinealy observes that:

> The arrival of the blight coincided with a period of rapid

population growth and relative economic stagnation. The livelihoods of a large number of poor people were particularly precarious. For this group of people the blight could not have arrived at a worse time. A few decades earlier and dependence on the potato would not have been so acute; a few decades later and the economy could probably have made its own internal adjustments.[11]

Bardon notes:

> At the beginning of the 19th century poor farmers and labourers had supplemented their incomes by spinning and weaving wool and linen in their homes. The collapse of domestic industry left the vast majority of people in the congested countryside utterly dependent on the land.[12]

The poor impoverished peasants so dependent on the land were utterly destroyed when the blight – or *Phytophthora infestans* – hit the potato crop in 1845. From 1845 to 1847 the crop was ruined and the peasants were doomed to starvation. Starvation brought with it diseases and fever, such as typhus and cholera.

To go some way towards helping the poor, in 1838 the British government had passed what was known as the Poor Relief Ireland Act.[13] This act divided the country into districts or unions. In Mayo there were five unions, namely Ballinrobe, Castlebar, Ballina, Swinford and Westport. In each Union a workhouse was established and administered by an elected board of guardians, all accountable to the commissioners in Dublin. The cost of administration was to be covered by a levied rate on valued property. Foxford came under the Swinford Union.[14] A report by the Foxford correspondent for *The Connaught Ranger* newspaper in 1846 states:

In the villages between that town and the Pontoon, entire families are lying, and many of them are dying. Eight of one family are confined to the bed of sickness, their only attendant being a boy six years old. Several other families have no person to wet their parched lips, the neighbours being in dread to approach the cabins of contagion. The scourge has now gone forth, and what may be spared by one calamity will, we fear, be hurried off by another. Such is the situation of the poor while the rich are making no effort, by friendly contributions, to relieve the necessities of the people whose sinewy arms enabled [them] to fare sumptuously every day. Now they are lying low and their moans unheeded, save by the carrion crow, who perched aloft upon the top of dying knell of many hapless victims of fever and starvation. God of mercy, receive their souls into thy glorious kingdom. May their transit from this world be a happy one.[15]

In 1845 the report of the chairman of the Foxford relief committee, George Vaughan Jackson, read as follows:

On our way to Foxford Petty Sessions we observed a vast deal of destruction done by floods caused by a fall of rain within the last four days that in severity is almost unprecedented. At a place called Coolcronan the poor people met us on the road and showed us acres of potatoes that were entirely covered with water and ruined. We also saw poor creatures up to nearly their knees digging potatoes to save them. In some districts the population were obliged to leave their house.[16]

A picture of Foxford almost three decades later is painted vividly by Robert Greer, a former rector and a graduate of Trinity College, which shows little improvement from the time of the Great Famine:

It was in the partial famine of 1872 that I first set foot in the sad, struggling, soot-dropped village of Foxford. It was a short time before the rise of Davitt and Parnell. The village had then only a few slated houses, and those thatched were for the most part streaked with soot-rain, and showed little signs of limewash without or within. The shops were few, and no show or display could be seen on the little common-place windows. I don't remember any part of the streets being flagged or paved. The clergy found lodging as best they could. The Protestant church was, externally, such as it is at present, but within it was inglorious, lone, half white-washed. The Catholic Church was decrepit and small, and quite unfit in space, etc., for the crowds who assembled for divine worship. The one bright spot in the town that struck me was the River Moy in grand flow and the fine bridge of seven arches that spans it … [I]n the distance nestling amid the hills and heather, the glens and rocks, could be seen the huts, houses, and hamlets of the people; some white-washed, some the same hue as the rocks and heather around, and all built of loose stone fathered from the immediate hill and moorside … The dawn arose in Foxford and shed its light into the soot-dropped cabins and into the saddened lives therein, and this village, amid the bogs and mountains, began to rejoice and blossom as the heather all around. In the early nineties the mills were started by a Working Order of the nuns … I had the pleasure of conversing with the Venerable Revd. Mother of the Providence Convent, Foxford in the room of the once little home where her great life-work began. The lady, though somewhat bent with the weight of four-score years, and with the burden of anxious care that her great work entailed, yet in aspect, tone, and converse shows the great heart and brilliant mind ever essential to do great things.[17]

In 1880 J. A. Fox, a member of the Dublin Mansion House

Committee, which was established for the relief of distress in Ireland, visited Foxford and recounted:

> In some of those hovels evicted families had lately taken refuge, so that the overcrowding added to the other horrors of the situation. In one house, in the townland of Culmore, there were four young children, one of whom was in a desperate condition for want of its natural food – milk, without which it was no longer capable of retaining anything whatever in its stomach. It lay on a wallet [*sic*] of dirty straw, with shreds and tatters of sacking and other things covering it. The mother was in Foxford begging for relief, the father being in England. In no Christian country in the world, probably, would so barbarous a spectacle be tolerated except in Ireland.[18]

In a return visit to the town Mr Fox stated, 'We found that there was no dispensary doctor in the town, the nearest doctor was located in Swinford, a distance of eight miles.' He also ascertained that thirty people in the area had been recently diagnosed with fever, yet none of the infected houses had been disinfected by the relevant authorities. Typhus, or famine fever, it was opined, was the chief cause of death rather than hunger, as the food situation worsened. This distress, compounded with cholera among pigs and chickens, left large sections of Mayo destitute.[19]

Dr Sigerson and Dr Kenny of the Medical Commission of the Mansion House Committee recorded:

> In the Foxford district, we have seen several convalescent cases, and some still suffering. Before leaving the latter locality the discovery of certain other cases of typhus fever was reported to us. It should be added that disorders other than typhus

fever may result from insufficient nutrition. Gastric troubles of various kinds may first show themselves. Then at a more intense degree come dysentery, diarrhoea, and typhoid of which we found numerous examples in the Swinford and Foxford districts. The history of the cases uniformly showed that the sufferers, children in most instances, had been compelled to subsist for a long time on Indian meal porridge, without milk … [W]e desire to see a more common use of disinfectants, to prevent spread of fever by infection.[20]

Add to this situation, little or no employment, a lack of education and little or no leisure or social activity, and one is looking at the bleakest conditions imaginable for human survival. Rev. T. A. Finlay, writing in the *New Ireland Review*, describes conditions as follows:

The manure heap was at the doorstep. In wet weather you had to pick your way to the door across a line of stepping-stones through a black evil-smelling pool. Disease was bred at the very doorposts; typhoid fever became an epidemic whenever the weather favoured the development and diffusion of its deadly germs. Within the house the cattle, and worse still, the pigs occupied a large portion of the dwelling. How the human inhabitants contrived to bestow themselves at night was a puzzle to the visitor who had no experience of the devices imposed by this primitive housekeeping. As a rule, in the single apartment which sufficed for parents, children and livestock, only one bed was visible. This could hold only a few members of the large family; how did the remainder take their rest? And in the too frequent times of sickness, when the bed was occupied by one or more invalids, how was provision made for those still in health? What ingenuity was required to solve these problems only those who studied them on the spot could realise.[21]

W. L. Micks observed that:

> Nothing would have enabled a stranger to realize the conditions
> of home life as well as visits to the cottages or in many cases,
> hovels, after nightfall when there would be found in the small
> unventilated structure all the members of the family with cattle,
> ponies, pigs, and poultry. A stranger would be disgusted and
> would wonder why people choose to live in such conditions. It
> was not the people's choice.[22]

Tim Pat Coogan states:

> In Mayo, there were few roads to speak of. Access to the
> clusters of swarming mud cabins, known as clachans (too small
> to qualify as villages), meant negotiating reeking mounds of
> animal, vegetable, and human waste girding the cottages. In
> the circumstances one can understand O'Connell's amazement
> at the health of the people. Hygiene was not a priority in
> nineteenth-century Ireland. Some good came out of the
> mounds of waste because they could be used as manure.[23]

Conditions, though somewhat improved by late 1900, still
remained such that a tour of northern Connaught in late 1900
by George Wyndham, chief secretary for Ireland, was reported as
a 'tragi-comedy'. Biggs-Davison quotes from a letter of George
Wyndham to his sister Madeline:

> And so we bumped round going into the cottiers' wretched
> hovels. No one knows in England what 'Hell or Connaught'
> means. Here was the real Irish question and all the Nationalist
> remedies of confiscation and compulsory sale would only
> stereotype an intolerable existence … [O]ne home had a family

of five in one room 11 feet by 7 feet. In the other room a family of seven. It was complete and picturesque, stooping to get under the lintel and waiting till your eyes could pierce the peat-hags there slowly emerged to sight – a hand loom; the pig; the cow and the manger; the donkey; the bed; a rocking cradle with a child; the heart; the spinning wheel.[24]

The Famine left a profound mark on the Irish psyche, discernible to this day. Some analysts say that it produced a kind of inner melancholy and fatalism, different from the earlier, more light-hearted spirit of even the poorest Irish. It created the tradition of mass emigration that has affected Ireland so deeply.

> [Emigration] intensified the old sense of bitterness against the English. Some of the emigrants even talked of 'genocide' believing that the English had deliberately provoked the Famine. This is not true: it was *laissez-faire*, not genocide.[25]

Over the period 1841–1851 the population of County Mayo fell by 29 per cent, from 388,887 to 274,499. Death and emigration were the legacy of the Famine, and these two factors drastically reduced the population of the West of Ireland.

After the horror of the Famine, the Land War came into play. Bernard O'Hara writes:

> After the Famine, social conditions began to improve in rural areas with some farmers able to increase the size of their farms and so create a more economic holding. By the late 1800s almost all of the land was owned by a small number of large landlords. The conditions of agricultural labourers, however, improved very little with most living in poverty. There was continuous friction between landlords and tenants, as well as agricultural labourers,

resulting in crimes known as 'agrarian outrages' which involved writing threatening letters to murder.[26]

Landlords used eviction to rid themselves of the low rents. Poor families and their measly belongings were thrown onto the side of the road, while they watched in horror as an implement known as the 'Battering Ram' tore apart their humble dwelling. Michael Davitt, from Straide, a small village only a few miles from Foxford, had first-hand experience of these events. In 1850, at the age of four and a half, he saw the power of the landlords and what they could do to families who could not afford to pay the high rent. In his book *Jottings in Solitary* he describes the scene:

> [Failing] to wipe off all arrears, [we] were one morning thrown out on the roadside and our little house and home pulled down before our eyes by the reigning institution: the 'Crowbar Brigade'. I was then but four and a half years old yet I have a distinct remembrance (doubtless strengthened by the frequent narration of events by my parents in after years) of that morning's scene: The remnant of our household furniture flung about the road, the roof of our house falling in and the thatch taking fire, my mother and father looking on with four young children.[27]

Bernard O'Hara records:

> The family made their way to Swinford workhouse, but under the workhouse regime, male children over three years of age had to be separated from their mothers. On hearing this, Catherine Davitt left the workhouse willing to take her chances on the roadside. The family spent no more than an hour in the Swinford workhouse, but Martin Davitt, Michael's father could never bring himself to refer to the event such was his sense of shame.[28]

This scene stayed with Davitt throughout his life and it was to mould his thoughts and actions in the future. To try to help the peasantry of the county, in August 1879 Michael Davitt founded the Land League of Mayo, at the Imperial Hotel in Castlebar. The organisation was a forerunner to the Irish National Land League, which was established in October of the same year. The aim of the Land League was to achieve fair rent, fixity of tenure and free sale, commonly referred to as the three Fs. Davitt was insistent that a fair rent be implemented by the landlords, and he urged farmers to pay no rent until they got a substantial reduction or were offered what was deemed to be a fair rent. *The Connaught Telegraph* newspaper carried Davitt's speech:

> as he now called upon them, to look to their interests and the comfort of their homes first, and then give the landlord a rent that they could spare. Now they had triumphed over the Government of England and the landlords of Ireland, and by their action they had made the landlords the weaker party – then in the name of reason, justice and common sense, let the landlords go to the wall.[29]

William O'Brien, a journalist from Mallow in Cork, and a friend of Davitt, had resigned his Cork City parliamentary seat and had settled near Westport in 1891. He had written some articles on the West for *The Freeman's Journal* in 1879, but the crisis condition he observed in Mayo prompted him to end his retirement and to champion the cause of the small farm holder. Fergus Campbell writes the following:

> It would take a hard crust of selfishness, indeed, to enable a man to settle down in the Mayo of that day without being shocked by its sorrows and incited to redress them. Every other year the

turf harvest was ruined in June or the potato harvest in August, and wan faces presented themselves at the windows, and humiliating begging appeals had to be set going to prevent semi-starvation from going the whole length of its ravages amidst the swarming villages. It was impossible to live long in Mayo without seeing that the remedy was as luminously self-evident as the disease: that while the overcrowded villagers ... lived on patches of heather hills ... these scenes of wretchedness were surrounded by wide-ranging pastures, from which the villagers or their fathers had been evicted in the clearances following the Great Famine of 1847, of a Big Grazing Plantation.[30]

James Laffey recorded that:

In the years after the famine and during the land war, the population of Foxford increased as more and more people descended on the town to escape the poverty and hopelessness in the neighbouring villages.[31]

However, some remained until they were evicted and then went in search of shelter wherever they could find it.

The Establishment of the Foxford Woollen Mills

AGNES HAD FIRST toyed with the idea of establishing a woollen mill while she was living in Ballaghaderreen. Before leaving there she paid a visit to a mill, at Collooney, County Sligo.

> Knowing there was a Woollen Mill at Collooney we thought well of inspecting it, and a few weeks before moving, accompanied by Srs. M. Benitus Brennan and M. Magdalen Segrave, we went by an early train to call on Mr. Sims. His manager Mr. Greer was most civil and told us everything, however we realized that it was but a small affair compared with our ambitious notions.[1]

She was not the first person to see the opportunity this industry presented for the region. As far back as the end of the eighteenth century, William Preston stated that:

> In the Province of Connaught the linen industry was making rapid progress and three great linen marts were flourishing in the towns of Westport, Castlebar, and Ballinrobe. The woollen manufacture is particularly suitable to the country, as like linen, sheep can be reared and maintained almost anywhere, and the mountainous parts of the country are very suitable, moreover it is an industry in which plenty of employment can be given.[2]

This account of the linen industry thriving in Foxford is substantiated by Marcos Aguinis, who says:

> Foxford had 144 looms, all part of Ireland's once-thriving textile industry. The mills were strung along the banks of the River Moy, whose fast-flowing currents propelled their huge wooden wheels. Their success did not suit the occupying authorities, however, and the British government moved to restrict the operation of woollen, and later linen mills in Ireland. In effect, it legislated to create poverty. One after another, the giant wheels stopped turning and from many towns and villages, including Foxford, people started emigrating to the United States of America, leaving behind the mills, still and sombre, as memorials to a once-thriving industry.[3]

In Foxford, Agnes discovered that all the necessary raw material was at hand. The power of the River Moy, which flowed through the town on its journey to the sea at Killala, could be harnessed to turn the turbines of the mill. Agnes, on seeing the majestic river for the first time, knew that 'in this powerful river was the source that she needed to power her project'. This was the most crucial element in establishing the industry. Secondly, the wool could be got from the sheep that were reared locally. The farmers would have an income through selling the wool to the mill. There would be no huge cost involved in transport or carting fees, as the farmers could bring the wool directly to the mill by horse or donkey and cart. The third element needed for the project was labour, which was readily available in the area. The men and women were crying out for work, and this would be a welcome opportunity to earn a weekly wage that would alleviate some of the poverty and hardship they suffered. It would give the people self-esteem and a sense of working towards a goal. It would also foster unity, which was sadly lacking in the region.

The next question for Agnes was how she should go about achieving this goal. However, she had an unwavering belief in Providence and often mentions this in her notes.

Fr T. A. Finlay described Agnes's plan:

> It was at once novel and daring, had in it that element of apparent rashness which characterises the ventures of missionary pioneers. In medieval times, when agriculture was the main industry of the nations, religious communities took a prominent part in promoting the material interests of the people; the monks were successful agriculturists, and the benefits of their labour diffused themselves largely around settlements. But in the new industrial order created by the inventions of the eighteenth century the religious community found no place. The organisation of manufacturers on a large scale, the operations of purchase and sale in distant markets, the complicated processes of exchange – all this was taken to be incompatible with the limitations imposed by the religious life. A more serious hindrance still: the life of the cloister gives no facilities for the training of the entrepreneur – the captain of industry; and without the guidance of the skilled leader the industrial army is ineffective in the field of modern competition. But in industry, as in literature, genius can supply the place of education, and in the case of the organiser of the Foxford enterprise this substitute was available.[4]

Agnes and the Sisters set things in motion to begin this daunting enterprise. Gildea writes:

> Sister Columba Feeney, one of the Sisters in Foxford, sought the advice of her cousin Michael Davitt, the Land League

founder, who was born in Straide just a few miles from Foxford in 1845. Davitt and his family were evicted from their humble homestead, and if any man knew the ravages of poverty on his countrymen and women he did, so no doubt any help Davitt could give the Sisters he would. He referred her to Mr. Peter White, manager of his Woollen Company in Dublin who, in turn, referred her to John Charles Smith, of Caledon Mills in Co. Tyrone. Agnes wrote to Smith explaining her idea of starting a woollen mill to relieve the destitution in the area. On acknowledging her letter, he asked her 'was she aware that she had written to a Protestant and a Freemason'.[5]

However, as far as Agnes was concerned, this was not a deterrent. She was willing to embrace whatever it would take to better conditions for the people of Foxford. In the following account Margery Mary Butler sums up succinctly the challenge that faced Agnes:

> Nothing could be more in harmony with the spirit of Mary Aikenhead than the establishment through the zeal of her gifted daughter, Mother Mary Arsenius Morrogh-Bernard, of a woollen mill at Foxford in 1892. Heavy rents, overcrowding, and a notoriously sterile, inhospitable soil combined to make conditions in the village and its neighbourhood nigh intolerable. Poverty was a chronic evil which the local resources could never overcome. An industry of some size seemed to be the only remedy. So Mother Mary Arsenius determined that Foxford should have an industry. She was a nun without commercial training, and it was the end of the 19th century, the age of the new industrial order, of grimy factories, huge machines, complicated processes of exchange sale in distant markets, organisation on a giant scale. What did all that matter? She

would do her little part and God would do the rest. 'Providence will provide,' she was known to exclaim in every difficulty.[6]

In June 1891 John Charles Smith travelled to Foxford at his own expense. He was the owner of one of the leading woollen mills in Ireland and if there was potential in this venture, he would know. The following report appeared in *The Morning Post*:

One of the most successful woollen mills in Ireland is that which was opened in 1833 at Caledon, a small village situated on the borders of the counties

John Charles Smith.

of Tyrone and Armagh. They were founded by the late Mr. J. C. Smith, who secured the extensive flour mills belonging to Lord Caledon, cleared out the flour milling machinery, and introduced the complete plant of woollen mills. Mr. Smith was joined in the following year by Mr. W. Sherrard, who had been for many years the representative of Messrs. Stewart and MacDonald of Glasgow. The firm began by manufacturing Irish cheviots and homespun tweeds, and obtained within a short time a reputation not only for good and serviceable material, but for excellence of design as well.[7]

John Charles Smith was doubtful if the venture could succeed. He made the point that Arthur Guinness had failed to construct a wool factory on the Liffey, and he suggested that Agnes abandon the idea. The *Belfast News Letter* reported:

On the invitation of Mrs Morrogh-Bernard he paid a visit to Foxford. She did not find him enthusiastic at first. He was mistrustful of the project of the woollen factory founded and promoted by a lady. He had too large a knowledge of the difficulties which beset such an undertaking to lightly give his approval to the scheme.[8]

Agnes had not the least intention of abandoning her idea, and seeing her determination, Smith placed himself at her disposal in an advisory capacity for the rest of his life.

Mr Smith was not a Roman Catholic and could not be assumed to have much sympathy with the undertakings of Roman Catholic religious sisterhoods. But it was discovered that his sympathies were not at all of the sectarian kind, that he had a helping hand for any undertaking which promised to improve the social condition of the Irish en masse.[9]

Smith arranged training for the Conroy sisters at his mills in Caledon. The sisters had been with Agnes in Ballaghaderreen, and they had established a good relationship. Furthermore, Smith loaned her his trusted trainee manager, Frank Sherry, a Catholic, who would in fact manage the incipient woollen mills and was never to return to Tyrone. Aiden Quigley, Frank Sherry's grandson, quotes from Frank Sherry's notes:

When I left Tyrone, I left a fertile county where there was poverty enough, but not such poverty as can abound in an infertile region where there is no possible source of income but the unwilling soil … [Mr Smith] brought me to Foxford himself. We arrived at 2 a.m. on a December morning, and I saw the west first as snow-spread country, silent and lonely, set among high white hills. I wasted few glances on it for I was weary of the long journey … [A]fter breakfast we ploughed our way through the snow drifts to the mill, where the contractors were at work erecting a shed. To say that we came to the mill is putting it nicely – we really came to a place where, if God willed, there might one day be a mill. At the moment there was snow, slush, mud and one shed, plus the great spirit of a nun, backed by the approval of the Mother General of the Order, and a deep unquestioning trust in divine providence. That was December 1891.[10]

Frank Sherry.   *James (Jim) Sherry.*

However, on his first visit home at Christmas 1891, Frank persuaded his brother Jim to join him in Foxford, and they returned there after the holidays.[11]

Foxford was going to have a deep and lasting influence on the Sherry family, although they didn't know it at this stage.

Frank Sherry married Margaret Brennan, a 'ward' of Agnes's from her days in Ballaghaderreen. They had five children in family. In January 1949, Frank Sherry passed away at the age of 81, having been manager of the Mills for over half a century. He was succeeded by his nephew, Seamus, son of Jim Sherry. After

Seamus retired in 1982, another of Jim's sons, Kevin, became manager.[12]

At this time, Agnes's main concern was getting the finance to establish the mill. The Mother General of her order, Mrs Margison, agreed to mortgage their head house at Milltown, in Dublin, to guarantee a loan of £5,000, which Agnes needed to get the project off the ground. It was fortunate for Agnes that the Congested Districts Board had been established in 1891, as it would be this body that would provide funding for the project.[13] Agnes notes in her memoirs: 'By this time, we were keeping a sharp eye on the lately formed CDB, knowing that it had the handling and dispensing of large sums of money for the benefit of the Irish poor.'[14]

Agnes hoped that through her friendship with Charles Kennedy, a member of the CDB and one of Dublin's philanthropists, she would be able to secure the finance needed. She had applied to the Board for a grant early in 1892 but was still awaiting their response by the autumn of that year.

Another pressing matter for Agnes was advice and instruction on the setting up of this industry. In her notes from March she makes the following entry:

> I went direct to Milltown to borrow money and report to Mother General and Mr. Charles Kennedy. We arranged to meet next day at St. Vincent's. He brought me there and introduced me to Mr. Horace Plunkett and Mr. Tuke, both members of the CDB. Mr. Plunkett was deeply interested in the project and gave me £100 to spend as I thought fit amongst the poor. These ten days in Dublin were full of work. Different interviews – with Dr. Redmond; with Fr. C. McKenna S.J., and Fr. T. A. Finlay S.J., on our technical schemes; with Mr. Kennedy

working for a loan. We had bought a second-hand, horizontal boiler, and as it entailed a chimney being built I went to see some mills at Greenmount and also Clayton's to make enquiries and pick up all the hints and information I could extract from knowledgeable people. Then, with Mother General's approval, I constituted myself commercial traveller, went to Clery's, had the good fortune of meeting Mr. Peter White there, saw the head men, talked of our future firm, its prospects and solicited orders.[15]

This displays yet again Agnes's aptitude for business, her tenacity and her ever-present ability to grab any opportunity that presented itself.

There is a very humorous and shrewd entry in Agnes's notes regarding a visit to the mill by CDB inspector Henry Doran:

> Mr. H. Doran CDB Inspector came to look at the mill. He asked, 'is that all you are undertaking.' We said 'by no means' this is but a small beginning. The people here are most miserably housed, their standard of living is the lowest, we intend to change all that; better houses must be built, better stock and poultry introduced and the lands better cultivated; the cottiers taught to grow vegetables and fruit as well as the everlasting and often failing potato; the girls to cook, to make butter and many other things … [W]e did not tell Mr. Doran all we had in view, only just enough to show him we were not to be 'sat upon.'[16]

In a letter to Mrs Margison, Agnes states:

> It appears the CDB are now ashamed that you, a woman, have beaten them in generosity and done what they with their

thousands to spend would not face for the poor congested creatures.[17]

The Board gave Agnes her loan in November 1892:

A woollen factory at which 43 hands are employed has been opened recently at Foxford, Co. Mayo, by the Sisters of Charity and to this community the Board has advanced a sum of £7,000 at 2½ per cent. Interest repayable in 18 years by fixed half-yearly instalments. Similarly the same religious community has opened a knitting factory at Ballaghaderreen, Co. Mayo at which 92 hands are employed, and the Board has advanced £3,000 on like terms to the same community. Both these loans are secured by a mortgage on real property possessed by the Sisters of Charity in Co. Dublin. It is also under consideration whether both these factories might not be further assisted by Capitation Grants for boys or girls instructed in the respective industries.[18]

This was followed in April 1893 by:

a gift of £1,500 from the Board to the Foxford factory and £500 to the Balllaghaderin [*sic*] Factory 'in consideration of the valuable services rendered by the Sisters of Charity in developing woollen industries, and in providing technical instruction for a large number of children'.[19]

The Board agreed:

to allocate a sum not exceeding £4,000 to be paid in twelve quarterly grants not exceeding £333 6s. 8d. each, the grants to begin to accrue on the 1st of January, 1894. Payment is to be contingent upon the satisfactory condition of the woollen mill, and upon the giving of such instruction in the technical school as shall meet with the approval of the Board.[20]

The work progressed surely and steadily, with:

> machinery purchased, and John Charles Smith visiting Foxford to get things moving. The store had to be prepared, sheds of timber with felt roofing put up, and machinery ordered. Some secondhand looms were sourced in Ireland and England, and machinery was brought from Guinness's closed-down factory, and more from England.[21]

A report on the fledgling industry was carried by the *Evening Telegraph*:

> A still more difficult task has been begun by the head of the convent of the Sisters of Charity in Foxford, Co. Mayo, Mother Bernard. Aided by a patriotic Protestant woollen manufacturer in Ulster, Mr. Smith, this nun is starting a Woollen Mill in one of the most congested districts of Connaught. It is in Mr John Dillon's constituency, and is two miles from where Michael Davitt was born.[22]

The mill was officially opened on 25 April 1892, just over a year after Agnes and her Sisters first came to Foxford. Sir Horace Plunkett and Charles Kennedy, members of the CDB, set the first loom in motion.[23] What a day for Agnes and her Sisters and indeed for the people of Foxford and its hinterland! What a joy it must have been for Agnes on that morning to experience the fruition of everything she had envisaged.

When the famous factory bell rang for the first time, twenty people took their places behind the looms. That inaugural bell was the harbinger of a promising new era in Foxford's history.[24]

The first order on the books was placed for the Baroness Burdett-Coutts. In a letter to *The Freeman's Journal* John Charles Smith recalled that:

> Baroness Burdett-Coutts ... has ever since taken a deep interest in the undertaking, and hundreds of yards of beautiful costume cloth have been sent to her recent orders, giving satisfaction to the lady and gaining credit for the staff of mill-workers. It may be here stated that when Mr Burdett-Coutts first visited and started the mill he was desirous of presenting a suitable souvenir of his visit, and requested me to procure four handlooms of modern construction for the Lady superior, on which she could have the poor peasants taught to weave in their cottages. It was found, however, that in all the miserable district there was not one cabin, out of many hundreds, which would accommodate a handloom. Therefore, so far the Lady Superior is unable to avail herself of the kind offer of this English gentleman, who so kindly wished to help 'the industries in the West'.[25]

By May substantial orders for blankets were arriving. The technique and materials used are described by Rosa Meehan:

> The fleece was prepared and all the processing involved in producing the finished woollen tweeds and blankets was carried out in the mills. The wool from local sheep, known as 'mountainy wool' was used to produce the coarse tweeds. As the factory's products diversified, higher quality wool was imported from Australia for finer materials.[26]

*The mill advertised for wool
suppliers in the* Western People.

The mill provided the means by which the people could earn a living:

> The poor were enabled to earn their daily bread and at the same
> time given the opportunity of becoming worthy citizens of the
> city of God, for in Foxford, the material and the spiritual were
> always to go hand in hand.[27]

In 1892 the following was reported:

> Lord Houghton the present Lord Lieutenant has already given
> an order for a piece of tweed. Amongst other kind friends who
> have come to the assistance of Mrs Morrogh-Bernard in her
> most praiseworthy undertaking are Mr Burdett-Coutts and the
> Baroness Burdett-Coutts, the Duchess of Teck, and Princess
> Victoria, her daughter, who gave an order for some dress goods. [28]

Even though the mill was proving to be a success, there were many obstacles that Agnes had to overcome. One of those was when a local landlord and magistrate, Standish O'Grady-McDermott, of Cloongee House on the banks of the River Moy, objected to the erection of a small weir on the Moy, as attempts were being made to create a millrace on the river. This objection by O'Grady-McDermott posed a very serious threat to the survival of the industry, as without a proper millrace the water supply could not be regulated. Frankie Devaney recalled that:

> O'Grady-McDermott had the fishing rights on the river and he maintained that the building of the weir would interfere with the passage of salmon upriver. He took the Sisters to court and ordered that the boulder weir be removed.[29]

William Devaney, Frankie's great-grandfather, who was a worker at the mill, wrote to Agnes about removing the boulder weir, saying, 'Madam, I cannot get anyone to do the work.'

A letter written by O'Grady-McDermott appeared in *The Freeman's Journal* outlining the reasons for his insistence that Agnes and the mill authority remove the boulder weir. In reply, John Charles Smith voiced his opinion on O'Grady-McDermott's complaint:

> The reasons which that gentleman gives for or in defence of his action in ordering the temporary weir to be pulled away appear to be somewhat vague and far-fetched. What has the using of a raft in the river 12 months since to do with the pulling down of the boulder weir, which is used at present to divert a small part of the waters of the Moy into the millrace of the newly started woollen mills? Your readers will perhaps imagine that the course of the river has been seriously changed, and that

there is just cause of complaint on the part of the gentleman who writes so fully about the matter. If such was the case no business man could make any protest against his claims. What are the facts? There is room for 10,000 salmon to pass without even coming near the boulder weir ... [M]ay I inform your readers how much of the Moy water the Lady Superior (who has spent over £13,000 already in trying to give employment) has diverted from its course? Well, just enough to turn a small turbine wheel about forty inches in diameter, or, in other words from 2,000 to 3,000 cubic feet per minute, that is to say, about as much as would pass through an opening the size of a large washing tub. This looks like a small quantity to borrow from the mighty torrent which nature hurls over the Foxford Rock ... When the boulder wall was thrown into the river, in order to secure the small supply of water for the mill, Mr O'Grady-McDermott objected, and part of it was removed on the orders of the Lady Superior and the Lady said she would remove all when she had time to have a plan made and get a cutting through the rock to waters above the bridge, as the lease and plan of premises granted to her by the landlord empowered her to do this. The plans were made, and duly approved of by the landlord's people of business, and all was ready to cut the rock at the cost of some hundreds of pounds sterling. Then it appears Mr O'Grady-McDermott objected also to this scheme, and finally, by a letter from his lawyer, demanded that the boulder weir be removed forthwith ...

Let us hope, however, that Mr O'Grady-McDermott will reconsider all these matters and act in the kind spirit in which he closes his letter and permit, without trouble and of his own free will, engineering skill to point out a method whereby the waters of the Moy may be harnessed in the service of that wild, barren and congested district, through which they have flowed in idleness for centuries ... May I conclude with the wish, or hope, that not only on the Moy, but on every river in Ireland, we may soon see, not one, but many mills, bringing comfort, plenty, and happiness into the homes of our native land.[30]

In the end a new millrace had to be constructed. Agnes recorded the event in her notes as follows:

> A millrace also had to be made. In former days there had been a millrace on the other side of the river, the ruins of which remained, but that was of no use to them.[31]

The new millrace was a heavy undertaking. It measured 350 feet in length and was constructed along the river bank. Its construction proved to be an arduous and costly exercise as time and again the powerful Moy swept away the newly laid cement. *The Freeman's Journal* carried the following report:

> The fates thrust Mr Standish O'Grady-McDermott of Clongee across its path. The gentleman, who is lessee of a local salmon fishery, complained that his salmon could not go up and down the large and wide River Moy on account of the stream that was diverted to turn the mill-wheel, and threatened an injunction that would close up the mill and send the mill hands into the poorhouse. He had legal right and the chances were against boating him in the courts. There was nothing for it but to construct a new mill race which had to be excavated for a long distance through the solid rock ... For three months from fifty to sixty workmen have been employed every day blasting up the intensely hard archaic rock. The explosive used was tonite, and considering that the rock was quite close to the houses of the town, it is gratifying and much to the credit of Mr Greene and his skilled workers that no accidents occurred while the work was going on.[32]

The new millrace was opened, much to Agnes's and the workers' delight. She had successfully overcome another obstacle. *The Freeman's Journal* reported:

> Today the new millrace of the Foxford Technical Woollen Mills was opened. The entire cost of the new millrace mounts up to over £100. If a little of the courage, grit, and patriotism of the good Sisters of Charity were more general, we should have reason to be hopeful for the future of Irish Industries.[33]

The people of the locality and further afield had come to the rescue. Was this another intervention by Providence? Agnes had overcome adversity and her industry survived. O'Grady-McDermott reconciled any animosity that occurred between himself and Agnes. Eithne Brogan recalled that 'O'Grady-McDermott made his peace with Agnes before he died. He died tragically.'[34] An entry in the BMD Register for Mayo states that O'Grady-McDermott died in February 1897 at the age of 59.

For Agnes the work continued, with steady progress being made in each department.

Agnes decided she would stage the Great Connaught Exhibition in September 1895. Mr Smith was the original source behind this thinking, but perhaps some of the motivation for this exhibition may have come from earlier successes. A year before, Agnes had sent several exhibits of Foxford goods to the Kirkby Lonsdale Exhibition. Kirkby Lonsdale, a market town in Westmoreland, was a thriving hub of the milling industry. *The Freeman's Journal* carried the following report:

> The exhibition has grown out of an industrial movement started here by Mr. A Harris, of Lunefield, with the aid of the County Council … [T]he special interest of this exhibition for

Irish readers lies in the fact that the Countess of Bective, who presides over the enterprise, has been at much pains to form a creditable collection of Irish exhibits.[35]

The exhibition was divided into various categories and *The Freeman's Journal* goes on to report the success of the Foxford entrants:

> Kate Conroy, came first in Class 3 – The Hand spun wool yarn dyed, a hank, not to exceed 1lb in weight, £2 given by Mrs Arthur Foster. Class 3 – Hand spun and hand woven home spun (woollen) with pattern or twill for menswear. First prize 15s given by Lord Dunleath; 1. Mary Kennedy, Foxford. Class 4 – Hand spun and hand woven home spun (woollen) without pattern, for men's woven web of 10 to 20 yds. 10s. given by Lord Crofton. 2. Mary Kennedy, Foxford, Class 5 – Hand spun and hand woven home spun (woollen) with pattern or twill, for women's wear, web of 10 to 20 yds 15s given by Hon. A. Pakenham 1. Bridget McKenna, Foxford.[36]

Agnes and her staunch helper and supporter Mr Smith believed that the Connaught Exhibition would provide the publicity vital for the success of her factory. It would make Foxford Woollen Mills one of the most respected and fashionable brands in Ireland and England. A number of influential individuals formed the committee that organised the event. It included the Countess of Bective, Lady Clanmorris, Lady Ardilaun, Madam O'Connor, Madam McDermott and Mrs Perry Knox-Gore.[37] In her memoirs Agnes states that:

> Mr. Smith and Max Green drew up plans for sheds for the Connaught Exhibition. The big northern hall was put up at this

time and was used for many years to come. Mr. Smith was the originator of the idea of organising the Connaught Exhibition in Foxford. He realised its potential in furthering the industry. The danger of exciting jealousy in other woollen industries had to be avoided but Mr. Smith believed the exhibition would increase the demand for woollens and hence help all woollen industries.[38]

The event, which was opened by Lady Cadogan and presided over by the Countess of Arran, ran over three days. *The Freeman's Journal* stated that it was:

> one of the most completely successful exhibitions of the kind ever held in Ireland. It was attended by an array of distinguished guests including Lord and Lady Arran, The Earl and Countess of Fingall, the Lord Chancellor and Lady Ashbourne, the Lord Mayor of Dublin, Valentine Blake-Dillon, Sir Horace Plunkett. The Countess of Lucan, the Countess of Kenmare, the Countess of Bective, Lady Clanmorris, Lady Ardilaun, Madam O'Connor, Madam McDermott, Lady Perry Knox-Gore, and Mrs J. Talbot Power etc. The guiding spirit, however, and the originator of the important move, the first of its kind in the West, is Mrs Agnes Morrogh-Bernard, Superioress of the Convent of Divine Providence, Foxford, who, many of your readers will remember, succeeded in the face of the most disheartening circumstances, and at a cost of over £20,000 in establishing a woollen mill there. Almost 200 persons are now afforded constant employment in these mills, whose products for durability, style and finish have already taken a firm hold in the markets not only of Ireland, but Great Britain, America, and the Colonies. The district around Foxford is among the poorest and most congested in Ireland; and only those acquainted with the past condition of its poor can realise the change for

the better effected by Mrs Morrogh-Bernard assisted by the members of her community since their arrival there. The great object of the Poultry Show and Exhibition is to encourage attention to poultry and eggs, to foster cottage industries, and promote technical education. It is essentially for 'the poor' for the purpose of placing before them in a practical way, the possibilities of improving to a material degree their condition by their own industry ... Prizes are also offered to encourage excellence in the management of butter, the treatment of bees and honey, for the cultivation of vegetables, and a special prize open to all Ireland for the best sample of potatoes, not less than 14 lbs, forming part of a bona fide field crop.[39]

The Great Connaught Exhibition, Foxford, September 1895.

James Laffey writes that:

The exhibition was divided into various sections displaying vegetables, flowers, poultry, diary produce, crafts, homespun and textiles. Companies and individuals who regularly competed at other exhibitions were invited to exhibit their wares, with the promise of free space at the exhibition and free carriage from the railway station.[40]

Of the exhibition *The Irish Times* reported:

> Perhaps no more wonderful thing has ever occurred in the West of Ireland than the holding of the Industrial Exhibition in Foxford. It was said that never before in Connacht had there been gathered together on so small a platform, men of so many diverse opinions – Catholic, Protestant, Whig, Tory, Nationalist.[41]

The Bishop of Achonry, Dr Lyster, declined an invitation to attend. In a conversation with Agnes he said, 'Do you expect me to take off my hat and throw it in the air and shout for those people?'

Despite the success of the exhibition, the mills still faced serious financial challenges, so with this in mind, Lady Arran established the Foxford Industrial Fund and appealed in the national papers for financial aid. The following appeared in *The Irish Times* in February 1896:

> The friends of the Irish Sisters of Charity, therefore, appeal in confidence to all Irish people and to the large-hearted English public who are interested in the industrial development of Ireland to come to their help, and by even the smallest dona-tions, assist in placing this industrial undertaking upon a firm financial basis. Our Irish men have long been discussing the need of an industrial revival, but whilst men were talking women began to work, and if the public will but help this remarkable

undertaking, carried on, as it is, almost entirely by women, and which is having such a far-reaching influence for good in the West of Ireland, they will, indeed, be helping to solve a difficult question.[42]

Many dignitaries subscribed to the fund, including Horace Plunkett, Mr James Talbot-Power, Lord Arran and the Lord Chancellor. In a belated attempt to remedy the dismay caused by his earlier fit of pique, Bishop Lyster contributed £100. Agnes later recorded:

> It was generally supposed that a good many wires had been pulled and much pressure brought to bear on Epus Acha (The Bishop of Achonry) before so satisfactory a conclusion was reached.[43]

Further success followed for Agnes in 1897 at the Dublin Spring Show. The *Mayo News* reported:

> At the Dublin Spring Show, which opened on Tuesday at Ballsbridge, an attractive stand was that of Mother Morrogh-Bernard who exhibited Irish tweeds and friezes from the Woollen Mills, Foxford.[44]

As the mill became more successful, Agnes had comfortable houses built for the employees. By the time John Charles Smith died unexpectedly, in 1896, the woollen mill he had helped create was a viable venture.

> He had made no less than twenty-three visits to Foxford at his own expense, advised on the construction of the buildings, the selection of machinery, the purchase of raw material, marketing

of the finished produce, and he also advised the best method of bookkeeping.[45]

When news of his death reached Foxford, there was deep and genuine sorrow. Agnes was upset by this sudden and sad news. It was Smith who had helped her in her time of need. Indeed the following report summed up just what he had helped to achieve:

> When the Sisters of Charity in Foxford determined to erect woollen mills in one of the most hopeless of the congested districts, it was to Mr. Smith they turned to for guidance and assistance. The appeal was not made in vain and thanks to the help thus generously afforded, Foxford tweeds are able to command their price in the market. It is therefore owing to the man and to his co-operation that in a district where in the past the only subsistence was the money earned at the English harvest and the only hope emigration to America or to the colonies, every worker has now a brighter vista, and a fair day's wage can be earned for a fair day's work. Mr. Smith's brother is one of the members of the Athlone Woollen Company. The Athlone Mills have done much to make the city in which they are situated one of the most prosperous cities of the Irish woollen trade.[46]

A meeting of the traders was called, and the chairman, Major D. R. Fair, JP, delivered the address which was carried in the *Ballina Herald:*

> On learning of the sad news, the people of Foxford, convinced that an expression of sorrow for his death and sympathy with his afflicted widow and children, should go forth from them, at once convened a meeting in the Northern Hall, at which all the merchants and traders of the town attended. Among

those present were Major D. R. Fair, J. P., Rev. P. Conlon C.C., Messrs P. J. Coughlan, Michael Gaughan, Daniel Morrin, Peter Walsh, Michael Coughlan, John J. Boland, Thos Boland, John Knefsey, Thos Henehan, John Glover, Henry Neill, Robert Neill, Jas Gaughan, P. J. Jones, I. M. Sheil, Martin Gaughan, Matthew Mulherin, P. J. Hardy, Thos Gallagher … [T]he Chairman said – Gentlemen, I regret extremely the cause which has brought us together this evening, and I am sure all present join with me in that regret. A good and tried friend, a wise counsellor, indeed I may say, a benefactor of the Foxford Technical Woollen Mills has passed away … When the news arrived in Foxford this morning the feeling of regret was general, but by none will the loss be more keenly felt than by Mrs Morrogh-Bernard and the Sisters of Charity here. When the factory was being erected Mr Smith – himself being the proprietor of extensive and flourishing woollen mills in the North of Ireland – came down to Foxford and gave his advice and the benefit of his experience to the good nuns and assisted them in every way in his power. He did this voluntarily, and without one shilling remuneration. But he had the sincere thanks and gratitude of the Rev. Mother and the nuns, which I am sure he valued far more. Such deeds deserve to be recorded. Here we had a member of the Presbyterian Church coming down from the North and helping on the work of the Sisters of Charity in the West … To the widow and family of the deceased we beg to tender our most sincere and respectful sympathy.[47]

The employees of the mill were shocked and saddened by the news. This man had done so much to provide them with a livelihood, had staved off emigration and had ensured they would be able to stay in their native place and raise a family. The depth of gratitude to him must have been enormous among the employees. They too gathered to express their sympathy to Mrs Smith and her family.

The Irish Homestead was the weekly publication of the Irish Agricultural Organisation Society (IAOS), founded by Horace Plunkett in 1895. It carried the following report on Mr Smith's death:

It is with sincere regret that we record the death of Mr. Charles Smith, founder and owner of the Caledon Woollen Factory. It might seem, at first sight, that Mr. Smith's sphere of effort did not touch at many points the field in which the IAOS is labouring, but Mr. Smith was a many-sided man, and Irish industry in many shapes has lost in him a friend whom it will be difficult to replace. In no quarter of Ireland will his death be more sincerely mourned than among the peasant workers of Foxford and its environment. To them Mr. Smith has been a benefactor whom gratitude will long prevent them from forgetting. When the enterprise of starting a woollen factory amongst them was first begun, and such unlikely pioneers in the work as a community of nuns took up the task, the venture seemed vividly visionary to many a sober onlooker. But in reality it was not so visionary as it seemed. There was a great fund of matured experience and of sterling business knowledge behind the responsible founders of the woollen factory. Without this support it would have been folly for them to begin … [T]he experience and the business knowledge were furnished by Mr. Smith. With a disinterestedness which we do not meet every day in commercial life, he set himself to make the philanthropic endeavours of the Foxford pioneers a business success. He guided them in the construction of their buildings, selected for them the most suitable machinery, provided out of his own mills foreman workers, who could manage competently the several departments of the new industry, taught the new manufacturers how to buy and how to sell, and during the early stages of the factory's existence, when it was slowly and painfully training the neglected labourers of the locality into the ways of industrial discipline, watched over every step of its precarious progress, rejoicing in its success as genuinely as if the success meant wealth to himself. In all this he was a rare example of the degree to which devotion to the public good can efface distinctions of creed and party. Mr. Smith was a Protestant, and the community with whose charitable work he co-operated so cordially and so helpfully was a body of Catholic nuns. We believe it is a custom with communities of this kind to preserve gratefully the memorials of the benefactors who have aided them in their services to the poor. If this be so, it will not be a surprise to find that in the future which, we hope, lies prosperous before the Factory of Foxford, the name of Mr. Charles Smith stands ever first on the list of benefactors who have helped to make the factory a home of remunerative industry and a centre of social reform in the midst of this poverty-stricken corner of Mayo. For ourselves, we regard the death of a man like Mr. Smith as a national loss. He was of those who, without ostentation, by silent, practical devotion to the promotion of a great industry build up the nation's fortunes along with their own. A generation of men imbued with his qualities, working as he worked, earnest in developing the industry which they had taken up, and solicitous to help out of their misery those who had no industry at all, would change in brief time the face of industrial Ireland.[48]

Mr Smith's death portended the death of another close friend of Agnes's. She recalled in her notes:

Soon after Mr. Smith's death, another friend, Mr. Costello, the Parson died. The sisters then bought the house he lived in, which had been the property of Major Fair. Parson Landy did not approve and tried to prevent the nuns buying the house.[49]

Links between Foxford and Caledon have remained strong down through the years. Those links, which were forged in such a remarkable way through the determination of a Catholic nun and the fair-mindedness of a northern Presbyterian, two people who made the welfare of others their priority, remain etched in history.

The founding of the Woollen Mills in Foxford in 1892 had a huge economic, social and cultural impact on the town and its hinterland. In *The Educational Times* Miss Bremner, an English non-Catholic visitor to Foxford, described Agnes's philosophy on the industry she had established:

> Walking in the Community garden, the foaming Moy (Mary's river) always sounded in her ears. 'Try me, try me' it said quite plainly. What could it do, all this water power running to waste? It could turn a saw-mill, but here was little timber. It could supply motor power for a mill of some kind. Since the neighbourhood is agricultural, supporting large numbers of sheep, why not buy their wool from the farmers, start a woollen factory, and sell woven goods? The Rev. Mother mentioned the idea to a few people, and they douched it well with cold water. A very likely thing that nuns – women who are, and always have been, mere babes in knowledge of the world – could buy wool, manage a mill, when labour is so difficult to control nowadays, sell in the right markets. The good Mother and her senses must have parted company to think of it for a moment ... Clouds, opposition, difficulties arose on every side, but still Mother Bernard's faith made her calmly say, 'It is God's work; He must help his people.' The general opinion was that the nuns were fools, and the feeling of being opposed did not make the task of

these gentle women more easy. There is no need to lengthen the story. The Divine Providence factory has been a great success. It has been extended again and again till it bids fair to swallow up the Convent Garden; it is still far from an imposing building. It is £17,000 in debt, but then it has brought work and wages to more than a hundred people and has caused comparative wealth to flow into Foxford. There are numbers of workers who earn 15s. or 20s. a week, and that means wealth. Last year £2,600 was spent in the purchase of wool in the neighbourhood. They make blankets, travelling rugs, flannels, shawls, serges, tweeds, friezes, and other woollen stuffs. Their goods cannot be called low-priced, but those who like a good article for their money will not consider them dear. The nuns have an annual turn-over of between £8,000 and £9,000.[50]

The Rev M. O'Riordan paints a picture of Foxford and the change effected in the few years that the Sisters had been in the town:

In 1894 there was not a butcher's shop in Foxford; in 1897 there were three. There are more than 1,000 families in the district making a radius of five miles around Foxford, nearly all occupiers of plots of land, or rather rocks, of a few acres in extent. In 1894 there was a manure heap before every door, and hardly a manure heap is to be seen before a cabin door in all Kinnemany [*sic*]; flower beds have supplanted them; the chattels no longer lodge with their masters, but occupy houses of their own; several cottiers have planted orchards, and nearly all the district is dotted over with chestnuts, sycamores, firs, and poplars. In the Sisters' garden you will also find another branch of technical work – a co-operative creamery. People come and sell their milk to the creamery, obtaining ready cash in exchange. At first they were distrustful, and eyed the thing askance; the Sisters lost on the venture, because in their desire to do good they gave too big a price. But now it is an acknowledged success. There is a constant coming and going of small children with milk cans. The milk is made into excellent butter, and since the best and most recent machinery is used, the creamery affords an object lesson in dairy work. One skilled dairy woman, with three or four learners, is constantly engaged in the dairy work. A third branch of the nuns' organisation of Foxford labour is a large workroom where various employments are taught and carried on. A number of girls are busy shirt-making, several sewing machines being in use. There are a dozen knitting machines which turn out large numbers of stockings. Here is a girl busy making quilts out of waste woollen fluff, which is encased in the same way as eiderdown. Sister Hickey is in charge of this department, and it is popularly believed that however extraordinary a thing is demanded from the workroom the Sister will find some way of supplying the demand. A number of young girls – farmers' daughters – work in this room, in the dairy, or are pupil teachers in the day school. For these board and lodging is provided by the Community at a moderate figure.[51]

O'Riordan goes on to comment on the change of fortune the nuns have brought about in the area and on their courage and commitment to do this work despite much adversity:

The improvement has progressed during the past six years, and is going on now. The change appears all the stranger when we know that it has come without initiative or aid from either magazine writers or draft-scheme economists. Even the Department was not called into synod, for it did not yet exist. It is all due to the initiative and energy of a few nuns who rise at five o'clock in the morning, begin the day with about two hours at meditation and Mass, repress their individuality for the rest of the day by complete obedience to a Rev. Mother, and have committed themselves by vow to the life-long foolishness of 'shifting the human centre of gravity to a future existence' ... It is not my purpose to consider the work of those nuns in more detail; but what I have said gives me the right to ask Sir Horace if he can point to a single instance in which the Department, with its ample supply of public money, with its highly-salaried experts and professional economists, has wrought such a transformation in any district in Ireland as those dozen ladies of the 'unproductive classes' have made in Kinnemany [*sic*]? Economists and experts of the Department! You have plenty money [*sic*] at your disposal, yet you have nowhere in Ireland done such a work as that. It is time for the public to ask, why? Is it because you do not know how to do it? Or is it because you do not take the trouble to do it? There are many districts in Ireland at present as Foxford was eleven years ago. Allowing you the vast advantage of the public money which you control, so unlike Sister Bernard who, with her community, has had to work mostly with money borrowed, and with principal and interest weighing them down, will you take up any of those deserted districts and show us in a few years such a change made by you as that which the Sisters of Charity have made in Kinnemany [*sic*]? But if that does not come within the functions of the Department – and if it does not, I do not know what does – can you get any dozen ladies, with money or family influence at their back, living in the world, and acquainted with its needs and ways, who will face such a task, and work a transformation such as that which has been made by those nuns of whose incapacity you write by implication: – 'I personally do not think that teachers who have renounced the world and withdrawn from contact with its stress and strain are the best moulders of the characters of youths who will have to come in direct conflict with the trials and temptations of life.' If bishops should invite other communities of nuns to establish convents in the midst of those places, and if they succeed, as they have succeeded elsewhere, in bringing brightness and life to where there was desolation and death, will you see in their presence also only an increasing 'multiplication of costly and elaborate conventual institutions' which 'is difficult to reconcile with the known conditions of the country'? and many economists of a generation hence complain that the Foxford nuns have usurped a work which secular ladies would be glad to do, and could do it better? But the first thing necessary to do a work is to be willing to do it, and the best proof of being able to do it is to have done it. And as it is with women, so it is with men. Amongst the most un-business-like men I have known have been those who call themselves 'men of business'; they are often the Captain Bobadils and the militia-men of industry. It is often those of them who have never proved their work by doing it, or even by trying to do it, who prattle most platitudes about 'the battle of life,' and about the need and the way of training the youth of both sexes how to fight it.[52]

James Greer gave the following description of an earlier and present Foxford:

> Travellers from Ballina or from Foxford can remember the early 'eighties when there was a famine' or almost a famine, in the land; the old 'Protestant potato' having melted in the pits. How sad and desolate little Foxford then seemed in the distance amid the hill and heather and turf clamps. Now it looks so different with the smoke of prosperity curling into the mountain air; no evictions; no straining 'to pay the rent'; no horrible dread of process-server and bailiff; no heartbreak wailings at the little station for loved ones starting out to distant climes, to be seen no more; no 'spalpeens' crowding the carriages on the way to

England's harvestings; no young mothers with a string of ill-fed and ill-clad children on the way to join the father, who was fortunate enough to find work to feed them and clothe them. All this blessed change has been brought about by the Sisters of Charity and industry.[53]

Agnes's project was viewed as a wonderful feat not only by the local and national media but also by others further afield. A report on the Foxford industry appeared in the *Daily Chronicle*, a British newspaper of the time:

> They are proud of the fine quality of goods they turn out, and aim at keeping up to the highest standard of production. Above all things they desire an English market, for the English have money to spend, and their people are so poor. What a godsend the weekly mill wage is to their homes can scarcely be realised in prosperous countries, where paying work is abundant. Now the people occasionally eat meat … The enterprise of the Sisters does not end with the factory. They teach girls cooking, dairy work, laundry work etc., and encourage the people to rear poultry, superior breeds of fowls being given out to the peasantry by the Congested Districts Board.[54]

Another visitor, Mr C. S. Buener, penned the following account of Agnes and her work when visiting the town in 1898:

> The Reverend Mother is no ordinary woman. Possessed of a considerable fortune, a beloved only daughter, handsome in person and with marked social gifts, she chose the life of a nun, and joined the community of the Sisters of Charity, bringing her fortune with her. Moreover, she possesses great power over others; when she wills a thing, sooner or later that thing has

to rank as an achievement, however impossible it seems at the time, however much friends attempt to dissuade her; there exists in her so much overcoming force, such power over others, that mountains of difficulty are finally overcome. She is the first to rise, the last to retire to rest; she takes no flesh food or stimulants, eats very sparely, rests little, spends much time in devotion. The calm and composure of her manner is striking; she knows no haste, worry or undue anxiety. Needless to say the Sisters regard her with an enthusiastic devotion in which the whole neighbourhood shares.[55]

He goes on to report during his visit to Foxford that:

Bank books are now quite common in Foxford. I well remember the day I left when I was sitting at breakfast Sister Ministress came into the room with twenty or perhaps even thirty bank books and showed me how thrifty the Foxford people are becoming. It must not, however, be imagined, that Mother Bernard's resourcefulness and helpfulness ended with the establishment of the factory. That only began the social revolution she inaugurated.[56]

The woollen mill progressed steadily as training and expertise improved.

In 1905, 105 people were employed and turning a profit. Their flannels, tweeds, shawls, blankets and clerical cloths could be purchased from Arnott's, Switzer's, and Brown Thomas in Dublin.[57]

Another customer of the mill was a Colonel Blake of the Connaught Rangers. The following appeared in *The Freeman's Journal*:

Orders have come from most of the great Dublin houses. Switzer's, Arnotts, the Henry Street warehouse, and from many parts of Ireland and England ... Amongst the latest orders was one received through Colonel Blake, of the Connaught Rangers, for 2,000 pairs of socks for the regiment.[58]

In 1922 the following report appeared in *The Weekly Irish Times:*

Run at first at a loss, the factory is now paying its way, and its products which include blankets, flannels, tweeds, friezes, clerical cloths, scarves and hosiery – the ladies dress material being particularly beautiful both in texture and design – are now well and favourably known, and are equal to the best, which can be produced elsewhere ... No one who sees the young men and women of Foxford working in the factory could imagine that a few years ago there was not the remotest idea of technical training in the district. A race of keen, alert, and clever workers has grown up who are a credit to themselves and to their teachers, while the children, who crowd into the dairy, cookery, laundry, poultry-rearing, domestic training, handicraft, and other classes promise even better things for the future.[59]

The project was up and running. Great difficulties had been overcome. Agnes's faith in Providence had paid off.

The Congested Districts Board

THE CONGESTED DISTRICTS Board (CDB) was established under the Land Act of 1891, the same year as Agnes and her congregation arrived in Mayo. It was opportune for them that the CDB had been established, as it would be the main source of funding for their fledging industry.

> The CDB was established as part of 'Constructive Unionism', a policy that aimed at 'pacifying' Irish agrarian unrest by a combination of coercive and conciliatory measures.[1]

In other words, according to Hickey, 'killing home rule with kindness'.[2] The issue of Home Rule dominated Irish politics between 1870 and 1920, although it became less of an issue with the outbreak of the First World War. Its objective was the establishment of a parliament in Dublin to legislate for Irish domestic affairs. This policy was devised by Isaac Butt, an Irish barrister, politician, and member of parliament at Westminster. Butt argued that 'Ireland suffered not so much from bad government, but from scarcely any government at all.'[3]

In making the concept of Home Rule attractive, Butt created a form of consciousness that was to shape the future of both the land question and nationalism. He argued:

> The heart of Empire beat too remotely from Irish grievance and

that MPs in the Imperial Parliament at Westminster understood little of Irish problems and were not willing to spend sufficient time considering them or trying to solve them. A Home Rule parliament in Dublin would understand, address, and solve Irish problems.[4]

Arthur Balfour, the Chief Secretary, visited the West of Ireland in the winter of 1890 and saw for himself the dire poverty and condition of the people. He realised something substantial had to be done to alleviate this. In this he was influenced by the findings of the Cowper and Allport Commission, established by Lord Salisbury in 1886, which:

> stressed the need for concerted state action to address the problems in the West of Ireland. Also, it deemed it necessary that greater state involvement should feature in order to develop an economic infrastructure, including railways, facilities for deep sea fishing, tramway construction and more labourers' housing.[5]

Arthur Balfour.

Balfour was influenced firstly by Ulster Liberal Unionist Hugh de F. Montgomery, who sent recommendations to him regarding the congested districts, and secondly by Mr William Micks. Micks, a local government inspector, provided Balfour with a number of sample family income and expenditure budgets from across the region.[6]

> These budgets, combined with the scenes of human misery Balfour witnessed, deeply influenced his decision to establish the CDB in order to break the perpetual cycle of grinding poverty.[7]

So in summarising his policy, it could be said that:

> Personal conviction, official recommendations, and Liberal Unionist pressure stimulated Balfour to advocate a considerable amount of state paternalism in his Land Act of 1891.[8]

CONGESTED DISTRICTS 1892

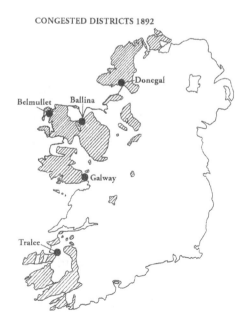

Congested Districts area in Ireland.

However, Balfour was of the opinion that despite all the poverty-relieving methods initiated:

> Permanent economic improvement for the West would come only when the Gaelic culture still predominant in the area was eroded by complete anglicisation of language, education, and cultural values.[9]

The first part of the Land Act provided an additional £33 million for purchase loans; the second part dealt with the problems of the impoverished West:

> This Act conferred upon the CDB powers of compulsory purchase to facilitate the amalgamation of smallholdings into economically viable units. The CDB aimed to deal with rural poverty specifically in counties along the Western seaboard, those of Donegal, Sligo, Mayo, Leitrim, Roscommon, and Kerry.[10]

The CDB sought to rectify socio-economic problems, which in some areas were identical to those that had prevailed at the time of the Famine of the 1840s. The problems they encountered included the absence of any kind of industrial production, a continued over-dependency on the potato and a high density of population, with early marriages and a high fertility rate.

Funding for the CDB came from various sources. The Irish Church Act of 1869 had disestablished the Church of Ireland.[11]

> Gladstone initiated this to 'pacify' Ireland, thus removing a major grievance for Irish Catholics, who were forced to contribute for the upkeep of the Protestant clergy. The property of the disestablished church was taken over by a Church

Temporalities Commission, whereby it sold church property and compensated clergy for loss of income.[12]

Part of the CDB's income was £41,250 a year, being interest at 2¾ per cent on the sum of £1,500,000, referred to in the Church Act as 'The Church Surplus Grant'.[13] The remaining monies were to be spent on charitable works in Ireland.

Another source of finance for the CDB was the Irish Reproductive Loan Fund.[14] This fund was a micro-credit scheme set up in 1824 to provide small loans to the 'industrious poor' and it amounted to £66,000 in securities, cash and outstanding loans.

> However, some of these funds were restricted, subject to the proviso that the moneys shall be applicable only to any county where the Fund might have been applied before the passing of the Act.[15]

Local associations and committees administered the scheme, most often from a small town in a rural area, and county committees oversaw their work. This fund was already allocating money to help the fishing industry in Cork, Kerry, Galway, Mayo, Sligo, Leitrim and Roscommon. In Mayo the following areas were served by the fund: Ballina or Carramore, Ballindine, Ballinrobe, Castlebar, Claremorris, Kilmore and Swinford. The CDB was limited in the dispersal of the Irish Reproductive Loan Fund.

The Board also received an income from a portion of the Sea and Coast Fisheries Fund, which amounted to about £18,000. Both the Reproductive Loan and the Fisheries Fund were considered 'purely Irish', as the money was collected by public subscriptions in London in 1822 for the relief of distress on the Irish western seaboard.[16]

The Board was permitted to accept gifts of property or money. It received as a gift the sum of £2,500, a portion of the unexpended balance of the Irish Distress Fund, subscribed in 1891 at the suggestion of the Earl of Zetland and the Right Hon. A. J. Balfour.[17]

George Wyndham.

Chief Secretary for Ireland George Wyndham was responsible for the introduction of the Land Purchase (Ireland) Act (1903), also known as the Wyndham Act. This ushered in the most radical change in history in Ireland's land ownership. Before, land was largely owned by landlords; within years of the Act, most of the land was owned by the former tenants, who had been subvented in their purchases through government subsidies. This was radical because:

> It differed from earlier legislation which initially advanced to tenants the sum necessary to purchase their holdings, repayable over a period of years on terms determined by an independent commission. The Wyndham Act ended the power of landlords

over tenants and made it easier for tenants to purchase land, facilitating the transfer of about 9 million acres up to 1914.[18]

Following the introduction of the Wyndham Act, the CDB was authorised to purchase extra land from large estates to enlarge the smallholdings of tenants.

Augustine Birrell, who was Chief Secretary for Ireland from 1907 to 1916, introduced the Land Purchase (Ireland) Act 1909, extending the 1903 Act and allowing for the compulsory purchase of tenanted farmland. In 1909 the CDB was granted compulsory powers of purchase and began redistributing over 1,000 estates, totalling 2,000,000 acres.

The Land Commission was another body responsible at this time for redistributing farmland in Ireland. It was initially established as a rent-fixing commission, under the Land Law (Ireland) Act 1881.[19] With the Ashbourne Act 1885, it developed into a tenant-purchasing commission and assisted in the agreed transfer of freehold farmland from landlord to tenant.[20] This was a response to the Land War, which had started in 1879.

> It was rapidly enacted by the government of Lord Salisbury, and was funded initially with £5,000,000. In all, under these pre-1921 Land Acts over 316,000 tenants purchased their holdings, amounting to 11.5 million acres.[21]

On the formation of the Irish Free State in 1922, the Land Commission was reconstituted by the Land Law (Commission) Act, 1923, which also dissolved the Congested Districts Board. Its staff was absorbed into the Irish Land Commission.

> With certain exceptions, the Irish Land Commission was authorised to compulsorily purchase untenanted land situated

in a congested district, or elsewhere if necessary, and redistribute it to relieve congestion.[22]

Terence Dooley notes that:

> This was a radical in Irish land policy, the object being the creation of economic farms. The Land Acts of 1923 were notable, in that the cost of land purchase for 114,000 tenants amounted to £30 million.[23]

A most important step was the Hogan Act, officially the Land Act of 1923:

> under which all land, where landlord and tenant had a dual interest, would be taken over by the Land Commission to be vested in the tenants subject to the payment of annuities. There would be no more haggling with landlords over prices, since a system of standard prices was introduced.[24]

The Land Act of 1933 was intended to expedite the compulsory acquisition and redistribution of lands. It empowered the Land Commission to redistribute any property it found suitable, with the exception of ordinary owner-occupied farms. This prevented landowners from laying claim to outlying farms as they had done in the past, because the Land Commission could acquire the property of landowners who did not reside in its immediate vicinity or who did not use this property in the same way as an ordinary farmer. Practically all agricultural land was bought out from landlords.

> By the late 1930s the Free State Land Acts had succeeded in transferring the bulk of the 114,000 un-purchased holdings on three million acres for £20.8 million.[25]

In 1983 the Commission ceased acquiring land; this signified the start of the end of the Commission's reform of Irish land ownership, though freehold transfers of farmland still had to be signed off by the Commission into the 1990s. The Commission was dissolved on 31 March 1999 by the Irish Land Commission (Dissolution) Act 1999, and most of the remaining liabilities and assets were transferred to the Minister for Agriculture and Food.

The first formal meeting of the CDB was held on 2 November 1891 at 23 Rutland Square, Dublin. The original Board consisted of the Right Honourable A. J. Balfour as Chief Secretary (or in his absence the Right Honourable West Ridgeway as Under Secretary), Frederick Wrench, Esq., an ex officio member as a Land Commissioner, W. L. Micks, Secretary, Horace Plunkett, Thomas P. Cairnes, James Hack Tuke, John Morley, Charles Kennedy, Fr. Charles Davis and Bishop Patrick O'Donnell. Temporary members included W. Spotswood Green and William Peacock.[26]

In the following years prominent people were appointed to the Board. These included David Harrell of Ballaghaderreen and, later, the Kiltimagh-based priest Fr Denis O'Hara, Sir Henry Doran and Fr T. Finlay. The first task of the Board was to ascertain what constituted a congested district. The statutory definition of a congested district was when:

> The total rateable value of a district when divided by the number of the population gives a sum of less than £1.0s 3d for each individual.[27]

Baseline reports had to be compiled for each district by the relevant inspector, recording the receipt and expenditure of each family in the area. The compilation of these was a huge task. It took over a year to complete and it was almost five years before the reports were all finally published. The CDB provided funding for land for tenants, and re-distributed it in economic holdings. It spent a total of £2,000,000 on improvements to land, houses, farm buildings, drainage, roads and fences.

> It encouraged a wide range of cottage industries – bee-keeping, spinning, knitting, crochet, lace-work, carpentry, kelp-making. It paid for instructors to teach domestic economy, poultry-keeping, egg production, and horse-breeding. It provided funding for many of the woollen mills and [for] carpet manufacturing. Agricultural instructors were employed to advise farmers. It promoted the fishing industry, building piers, allocating grants to fishermen for boats and fishing equipment, and it introduced marketing strategies. The sales of fish more than trebled between 1891 and 1913.[28]

Henry Doran, who lived in Tavrane House between Kilkelly and Bally-haunis, was the CDB inspector under whose remit Foxford fell. In May 1892 he submitted a report of conditions in Foxford (see Appendix 4). He noted the enormous economic contribution by women at the end of the nineteenth century:

Sir Henry Doran.

> This contribution covered the full round of the agricultural year: assisting in the springtime; getting the potato and oat crops in the ground before the men left for the seasonal work (where it was the annual tradition to go to England and Scotland) cutting and saving turf and reaping, when necessary, in September,

before the men's return. In nearly all cases, the women looked after the cattle, sheep, potato and oat crops, in addition to the more traditional women's work of tending pigs and poultry.[29]

Fr Denis O'Hara, parish priest in Kiltimagh and a close friend of Agnes, was also a member of the Board and a staunch supporter of its work. Kiltimagh, similar to Foxford, was an area ravaged by poverty. Like Agnes, Denis O'Hara was a champion of the poor and in 1897 he persuaded the CDB to adopt the Parish Committee Scheme which aimed at inducing tenants to make improvements in their holdings, dwellings and surroundings with the help of small money grants. Some members of the committee were elected and others were ex officio, such as clergymen, Poor Law Guardians and landlords. The scheme was a great success and this was duly noted in the records of the CDB:

> No one can pass through the districts in which these committees have been at work without noticing on all sides the new by-roads, extensive drains, and numerous small buildings with galvanised roofs which attest the success of the scheme and show that a real awakening of energy and industry has commenced amongst the small farmers and cottagers.[30]

Fr O'Hara's scheme, like Agnes's in 1893 to provide technical instruction in Kiltimagh, was approved by the CDB and was completed in 1895. O'Hara was described as:

> an ideal inland-country representative, as he had a thorough day-to-day experience of a toiling population living on small-holdings inadequate for the support of their families and whose men were obliged to migrate every year to England for harvesting work.[31]

The CDB also provided loans to the Lady Dudley Nursing Scheme, set up by Lady Dudley, the wife of the Lord Lieutenant in Ireland between 1902 and 1905, to employ nurses in the poorest parts of Ireland. Elizabeth, the Countess of Fingall, wrote:

> Lady Dudley mapped out a route where the Vice-regal car would pass the worst-looking cottages, outside of which the parish priest had been instructed to assemble the most ragged children. They even drove past the same cottage twice, and the chauffeur was instructed to slow down when passing. Ritchie was appalled, and George Wyndham got £12 million.[32]

The nurses were well trained and promoted cleanliness and healthy living.

> They were given a bicycle and equipped with surgical implements and medical stores. They were frequently called upon to set bones, dress wounds and perform operations. Thirteen such nurses were initially employed under the scheme, and in the absence of suitable accommodation the CDB provided loans to build houses for them.[33]

Five nurses were appointed in Mayo, with Nurse Daly appointed in the Foxford district.[34] Lady Dudley's committee continued to meet under her successor, the Countess of Aberdeen.

Support for the CDB was divided, some agreeing with its objectives, others more critical of it. It was accused of paternalism, of stifling, rather than developing local initiative. However, commendation for the CDB was forthcoming from many prominent people. Michael Davitt, in *The Fall of Feudalism*, praised Balfour's initiative in establishing it:

Though opinions differ as to the amount of good done by this body, there can be no doubt that much benefit has been conferred by its labours upon several districts comprised within the area of its operations. It has purchased a few estates and carried out improvements upon the holdings before reselling them to the tenants. The Lord Dillon estate in Roscommon and Mayo counties was acquired (1898) in this way, and the marked improvement that is now seen (in 1903) in the homes and the tillage of the small tenants on this property bear [*sic*] strong testimony to the excellent results of the board's efforts. The result causes much regret that the powers and income of the board are not adequate to the carrying out of large schemes for acquiring Connaught grazing ranches on which to 'plant' tenants with larger holdings and better land than the great majority of the Western peasantry live upon at the present time.

The power exercised by the congested districts board is that of an enlightened state socialism, and the credit due to the initiation of the plan of operations where its benevolent and practical work was most called for in Ireland, belongs to Mr. Arthur Balfour.[35]

John Dillon, who served as MP for East Mayo at Westminster, should have been opposed to the Board, as its work might threaten to kill off Home Rule.

However, he did not object to the work of the CDB in his constituency, as it was viewed as an apolitical entity. In 1897, he campaigned in the House of Commons for compulsory land purchase to be granted to the Board.[36]

Keir Hardie, a Scottish MP, visited Mayo in 1906. His purpose was to see at first hand some of the work of the CDB.

Accompanied by Fr Denis O'Hara, he visited a village in the hinterland of Kiltimagh. Hardie recorded the following account:

> The township of Cleragh occupied an eminence in the midst of a bleak, dreary moor. The owner of the holding was only able to support his wife and family by working for part of each year in England. Not surprisingly, emigration was a feature of the district; yet the practice of saving while in England or America was already well established and repatriates frequently settled in their place of origin, however unprepossessing the environment might be. This must surely be one of the mysteries, this love of home and kindred which deepens and grows in strength in proportion as the land is poor and the condition of life poor.[37]

On his return to Britain, Hardie described his fact-finding visit to Ireland. Even though he still considered the standard of living as poor, he saw some optimism. The following is his opinion of the work of the CDB:

> It is the most sensible institution I have ever known to be set up by law and with adaptions to meet differing conditions, forms the model upon which I would like to see our Unemployment Committees constituted.[38]

However, Joseph Lee, in his book *The Modernisation of Irish Society*, assessed the work of the CDB as:

> Far exceeding its promise ... the CDB invested heavily in uneconomic projects in the west of Ireland, projects that floundered once they stopped being subsidised. As a result, the flow of emigration from the West of Ireland was not converted

into internal migration to the more developed east, as might have been hoped.[39]

Sir Herbert Jekyll, secretary to Lord Houghton, the Lord Lieutenant between 1892 and 1895, had toured the West two years after the establishment of the Board. He wrote:

> The Congested Districts Board is doing excellent work, especially in fostering and extending the fisheries. Here again the difficulty is mainly with the people themselves, who in some districts do not take readily to seafaring life. Much has been done to overcome these prejudices, and much more may be done with patience and education. At many of the fish cutting stations men are constantly employed at good wages, while the fishermen find a steady market for fish which were formerly unsaleable … The extension of the railways has greatly benefited the fisheries, as it enables the fish to be taken to profitable markets.[40]

A letter from Colonel G. L. Tottenham of Glenade, County Leitrim, appeared in the *Irish Independent*. He was critical of some of the schemes allotted money by the Board, and he felt that they were of little use to the poverty-stricken people of the West. Part of the letter read:

> The spinning mule at Foxford worked by a turbine and with the assistance of two small boys does the work of 180 spinning wheels. From the point of view of the greatest amount of employment and diffusion of earnings, if there is demand for homespun at a remunerative price, how very far better it would be that these 180 spinning wheels should be at work in 180 scattered cottages, supplying numerous handloom weavers.[41]

Pauric Travers thought the Board achieved:

> considerable success and had an impact on the lives of those most disadvantaged in the congested districts. The accusations of state paternalism are somewhat misleading, in that its most significant features were its independence and its virtually 'amateur' status. It was an unpaid board whose members assembled monthly to decide where and how to spend its funds. Not until 1909 did any of the permanent staff become members of the board.[42]

Opinion on the work and politics of the CDB and its successor is summed up by Cormac O'Grada:

> Tensions lay behind the creation of the CDB and the Land Commission, but their ultimate resolution brought the landless and the western smallholder little joy. A less restrictive franchise before 1917 would have favoured the smallholder and farm labourer.[43]

Horace Plunkett, a member of the Board, was also the man responsible for the establishment of the Irish Agricultural Organisation Society (IAOS) in 1894, and was instrumental in establishing the Department of Agricultural and Technical Instruction (DATI) in 1889. Plunkett was appointed the latter's vice-president, which gave him control of the department's operations. He guided the policy and administration of the department in its critical first seven years.[44]

One of the aims of the IAOS:

> was to reduce the power of the small-town trader. Shopkeeper, publicans and butter-merchants detested the IAOS, though co-

operative activists probably had an exaggerated notion of the 'gombeen man's power to exploit'.[45]

The organisation rapidly became a powerhouse of co-operation, with thirty-three affiliated dairy co-operative societies and co-operative banks, leading to more economical and efficient management. Four years later there were 243 affiliated societies. Within a decade 800 societies were in existence, with a trade turnover of £3 million. The co-operative movement experienced its greatest success in the setting up of creameries:

> Plunkett got farmers to join together and establish these in order to process and market their own butter, milk and cheese to standards suitable for the British market, rather than producing unhygienic poor-quality output in their homes for local traders. This enabled farmers to deal directly with companies established by themselves, who could guarantee fair prices without middlemen absorbing the profits.[46]

His experience of being a member of the CDB deepened his conviction that the remedy for social and economic ills was co-operative self-help. His biographer reported that he believed:

> The only hope of real success for the CDB lay in the strict observance of the rule that a man should not, by state aid, be put in possession of a farm until it was ascertained that he was fit to run it.[47]

Plunkett remained a member of the Board until 1918. Underlying differences in philosophy meant that the relationship between the Board and the co-operatives were never entirely happy. Plunkett also made no secret of his wish to absorb the

CDB into the DATI. He claimed that there were congested areas in all parts of Ireland and that the problem should be tackled by a body that covered the whole country, such as the DATI.

> However, Balfour told Plunkett that while he was committed to merging the DATI and the CDB in the long term, nationalists would not accept the erosion of political and clerical influences within the CDB.[48]

While Plunkett appreciated the Board's good work, he was never happy with its undisguised paternalism.

A press report of a speech Plunkett made in 1890, advocating co-operative dairying to the farmers of Munster, led to a fruitful contact with Agnes's good friend Rev. T. A. Finlay, who had recently returned from studying the rural economy of Germany. Finlay, a professor of metaphysics at the Catholic University in Dublin, had edited important journals and held the position of professor of political economy at University College Dublin until 1930. Fr Finlay's influence on the co-operative movement, as well as on its founder, should not be underestimated. It was fortuitous that Plunkett and Finlay were to work so well together. Plunkett himself admitted:

> He largely moulded my life's work and was the kindest and most loyal friend I have ever had in a work which made my life worth living.[49]

However, Diarmaid Ferriter makes the point that:

> Plunkett's task ... was frustrating. He was a pioneer of the concept of systematic rural development, who, in spite of his

role in Irish affairs being often overlooked, influenced many international reformers, and can be credited as one of the few who had a long-term vision for the development of rural Ireland.[50]

Tensions often brewed under the perceived smooth surface of the political regime of the time, with P. J. Matthews noting that:

> Even though one could find liberal unionists, federal nationalists and separatists of various political hues willing to subscribe to the self-help ethos, political differences often boiled under the loose self-help coalition which emerged with the dawn of the new century.[51]

Whether it was coincidence or divine providence, in which Agnes always believed, the CDB was the instrument by which she furthered her goal. This organisation helped to establish an industry that was to be a lifeline to the people of the district. Horace Plunkett died on 26 March 1932, a few weeks before Agnes, in Weybridge, Surrey.

Another member of the CDB who was very influential on policies concerning the West was James Hack Tuke, a Quaker philanthropist and banker. He had visited Ireland during the Great Famine, accompanying W. E. Forster, another philanthropist, industrialist and Liberal Party statesman, on two journeys through the famine-stricken areas. In his book *Irish Distress and Its Remedies: A Visit to Donegal and Connaught, February, March and April 1880,* he urged 'land reform, promotion of local industries and the construction of light railways', all of which was adopted by the CDB. He was also a firm advocate of assisted emigration from the congested districts.[52]

Tuke, like Balfour and Plunkett, advocated state-funded

family emigration to relieve congestion.[53] Forster included a clause to this effect in the 1881 Land Bill. When Forster's incentive failed, Tuke organised his own committee, known as Mr Tuke's Fund, which assisted emigrants to travel to the United States and Canada.

Between 1856 and 1906, the Irish Poor Law Boards of Guardians also financed the emigration of about 25,000 paupers, primarily to the United States and Canada. In 1882–83 parliament passed legislation that provided for subsidies for the transportation of a further 54,000 emigrants. However, by 1884, due to opposition by the Irish bishops and others, the policy of assisted emigration was eliminated:

> The parish priests at first were passive in the matter, neither actively friendly, nor actively hostile, but some ten days ago Bishop McCormack of Ballaghaderreen in his Lenten Pastoral denounced emigration and the 'emigrationists' in the strongest language.[54]

For many of Mayo's poor, emigration was not an option, as they could not raise the fare for their passage. They were left at the mercy of the landlords. In truth many of the landlords were facing financial ruin themselves, and could not support their tenants. Donald E. Jordan notes:

> They were unwilling or unable as they were bordering on financial ruin themselves, as by law landlords were responsible for the levy for all tenants whose holdings were valued at £4 or less.[55]

This opinion is also expressed in the *Illustrated London News:*

The truth is that these evictions ... are not merely a legal but a natural process; and however much we may deplore the misery from which they spring, and which they so dreadfully aggravate, we cannot compel the Irish proprietors to continue in their miserable holdings the wretched swarms of people who pay no rent, and who prevent the improvement of property as long as they remain upon it ... it sounds very well to English ears to preach forbearance and generosity to the landowners. But it should be remembered that few of them have it in their power to be merciful or generous to their poorer tenantry ... They are themselves engaged in a life and death struggle with their creditors. Moreover, the greater number of the depopulators are mere agents for absent landlords or for the law-receivers under the courts acting for creditors.[56]

One might ask if killing Home Rule with kindness was politically effective. Finbar Madden states:

In one sense it was, in that the reforms introduced were long overdue and highly beneficial. However, in terms of achieving the ultimate aims it was a failure. The fact that close to four-fifths of the MPs elected for Irish constituencies continued to support the introduction of Home Rule would lead one to conclude that – despite the Government's best efforts – kindness had not done for Home Rule.[57]

Agnes the Fearless Campaigner

AGNES CAMPAIGNED ON behalf of many causes in her time, and she demonstrated her goodness and charitable nature in many ways during the course of her life. One such example of this is illustrated in a letter she wrote to Henry Doran, the CDB inspector, on behalf of a widow with five small children, who lived on a small farm that she was contemplating selling to pay off a debt. Agnes states:

> This would be a terrible mistake on her part, owing to her little family growing up. Therefore, in order to help her out of her debts and difficulties, and to assist her to keep the little farm until her children get older, we have offered to take the little holding for 3 years, leaving her a couple of acres for tillage and perhaps the grass of a cow, provided you will grant her this permission to sub-let under the circumstances. This would be a great act of charity. We would propose to give her a portion of the money each year in November. We are hoping that at the end of the 3 years she would be out of her difficulties, and be in a position to go on all right afterwards with her little family.[1]

Doran consented to Agnes's request:

> There will be no difficulty in having the object carried out in connection with the case but the letting must be of a character

that will not prevent her from getting an advance from the Land Commission for the purchase of her holding. For that reason I got the accompanying agreement drafted and if you will enter into it with Mrs. B the agreement will not put her out of legal possession and will secure the purpose you have in view so far as I understand it.[2]

Agnes must have been very pleased with her effort, ensuring that the family would have a means to earn a livelihood.

During the First World War she petitioned John Dillon, the MP at Westminster for East Mayo, for money for the poor:

The poor who live from hand to mouth are feeling severely the pinch of the war prices which are on the increase. Clothing, food and sickness are causing them much anxiety. May we rely on your usual kindness to help them this Xmas.[3]

And again the following year she wrote:

Our sisters who visit the poor meet cases of very great poverty in clothing, and bed covering. As you know, the prices of the household necessaries continue to be exorbitant. May we then ask your kind assistance to enable us to get them some Xmas comforts. An early reply will oblige in order to enable us to make timely arrangements.[4]

A note on the letter received indicates that £1 was received on 22 December. She wrote to Dillon again in 1923:

We will be grateful for your donation towards our Christmas Poor Fund. The continuous heavy rains and floods have left the crops in a sad condition. Where they were promising, now at best the yield will be but half a return. And there is no employment for so many who are looking for it.[5]

Here was a woman telling a man of some importance to send assistance in time for people to have some Christmas comforts. This shows her determination and strength of will, as well as her compassion for the poor. Agnes did not stand on ceremony with those whose help she sought. Care and consideration for the poor were her priorities.

Agnes's tenacity was again to the fore when she thought the valuation on the mill was too high. *The Connaught Telegraph* carried this report:

> Foxford Factory is valued at £5. In 1893 it was valued at £18 but this amount was reduced, and the local collector alleges that it was first valued at £30. Mother Morrogh-Bernard went to the valuation commissioners and got it reduced. The commissioners deny this, and now they are ordered to make a revision.[6]

Agnes took on this formidable group, questioned their authority, and achieved the result she wanted.

In 1896 the question of the establishment of a Belfast foundation arose, and Agnes and some of the Sisters went north to Belfast, with the idea of founding a convent there. In her memoirs Agnes records:

> We had been asked, what is to become of your young people when they are trained? Are they to emigrate? Are they to marry at home, and increase and multiply and fill the land and sow increased congestion? Can you make work for future generations? Our answer was, we want no emigration, already it is decreasing. Father and Mother and perhaps one or two of

their children are working in the Mill. See the comfort that brings into a house where comfort was never known before. That family wants no emigration; but the day must come when more willing hands will appear than work can be found for. That is why our thoughts turned to the North. Our young folk, highly-trained, knowing their trade thoroughly, would find work in the great Belfast Factories. With a house of our own up there, within their reach, we need have no fear for them, perhaps we could have a large Hostel as a Home for our girls, there would be ample work for us to do amongst them and others. Many influential friends were of our opinion and ready to help. The nucleus of a Fund was in waiting – Fr. O'Donoghue's Thousand Pounds which had come to Foxford and to Ballagh[aderreen]. and which Mother Catherine Norris and I, with his approval, had agreed to devote to this purpose. [7]

Agnes continues in her memoirs:

Mother M. Scholastica Lyons and I went North on November 4. We had a friend in Lisburn, Miss Armstrong, a Sister of one of ours at Foxford. (Sr. M. Allba). We went directly to her home. The following day she accompanied us to Belfast. We went to call on the P.P. of Ballymacarrett, who was expecting us. He received us with a warm welcome, gave us lunch, told us of all his hopes and projects, showed us the locality in which he hoped to obtain a site for schools eventually to be in our hands. Altogether things looked very promising. We were shown some of the Belfast Churches, the Falls, and other parts of the city, teeming with life and industry, and so back to Lisburn and next day to Dublin. On 8th, went again to Milltown to recap on all we had seen. I had offered to hand my work at Foxford over to another and go into the Black North if considered desirable.[8]

The CDB members did not approve of this suggestion and

neither did the Mother General. That the CDB would not approve of this plan was to be expected. Agnes was too valuable an asset to let go, and she had a lot of work to do in the newly established mill. The CDB was understandably afraid, in view of the loan that had been granted to the woollen mill, that if Agnes left the agreed repayments might not be honoured. Agnes confirms this opinion in her memoirs:

> The CDB were not at all in favour of me leaving Foxford for Belfast, in fact, they were opposed to it, on the plea that it is better to deal with the Devil we know than the Angel we don't know. For they had become accustomed to me and my ways and thought they were fairly sure of getting back the money lent us and of seeing some decent results from the grants they had made, as long as there was no change in the mode of using these monies. A new hand at the helm might not understand the sailing powers of the Little Craft and perhaps steer it into disaster. These men knew they were under the public eye. Some of their ventures had already suffered ship-wreck, and they had to go warily. Mother General wrote to the CDB giving her views and the decision she had arrived at, which was that for many years to come Foxford could absorb its own workers – that it would be more advisable to wait until the factory cleared itself and become self-supporting – that she had not at the moment a Sister trained to the work, to whom she could give the charge of the factory. She had not a Sister to spare who would be competent of organising the schools, which would be the chief work required in Belfast, and altogether that it was better to leave things in status quo. The CDB were content with that. So Belfast has been for many years on the shelf. The Sisters of the Holy Cross & Passion took up the position we had been offered and have done good work in Ballymacarrett. Still, Belfast is big enough for us all, and we go on hoping that in God's own time, he will call us there.[9]

The following extract is taken from *Watching for Daybreak: A History of St Matthew's Parish, Belfast*:

> Of particular significance in the history of education in St Matthew's Parish was the arrival of the Sisters of the Cross and Passion congregation in 1899 to build a new convent and hostel in Bryson St. The Sisters engaged in the good work of teaching and visiting, and also as a refuge for girls ... [T]he foundation stone of the convent and home of St Paul of the Cross, Ballymacarrett, was blessed and laid on Thursday 15th June 1899 by Bishop Henry. The advent here of this distinguished Order of religious has occasioned very great satisfaction and very Rev. Father John Macaulay, the revered pastor of Ballymacarrett, in establishing the good nuns in his parish, has accomplished an object which should further endear him to the hearts of the members of the congregation of St Matthew's.[10]

So another order of nuns was destined for the dream that Agnes had given some thought to. She never went to Belfast but stayed in Foxford for the rest of her life. But she had been prepared to turn over the mill to another and take on a new challenge in Belfast, doing whatever she could to improve conditions for students, workers and anybody who needed help.

Agnes left no stone unturned in the quests she undertook. She played a heroic part in the campaign for the beatification of the founder of her Order, Mary Aikenhead. Likewise, she spent many hours pleading the cause of her fellow Sister, Mary Charles Walker. Agnes was instrumental in bringing about teacher training for Catholic Sisters in the training colleges. She also advocated the teaching of the Irish language in these training colleges. In 1893 she wrote to Douglas Hyde, founder of the Gaelic League, in support of the teaching of Irish in schools. It was Hyde's belief that the nationality of a people found a fuller and truer expression in its own language and traditions than it could in any separate legislature, and for many years he succeeded in keeping politics out of the League.[11]

The Sisters of Charity in Foxford began learning Irish in December 1900. By the following May they were prepared to teach it as an extra subject in the senior and infant schools. In the autumn of 1902 the convent annalist recorded that 'Irish has been taught in all classes.'[12] Their efforts for the cause of the Irish language and Irish music were rewarded when in 1904:

> Douglas Hyde visited the convent school in Foxford to present medals and prizes which the choir had won at Westport Feis. He was more than surprised and delighted at the progress made here during the last ten years and made a long speech in Irish. He also presented the Sister who taught music with a gold medal in recognition of her untiring work in the cause of the Irish music revival.[13]

Agnes was vocal on the issue of primary and university education and she championed the rights of the children of the poor (see Appendix 3). She also fought with determination for the development of teacher training facilities for nuns. During her years at Gardiner Street and King's Inns Street in Dublin she realised that the teaching Sisters would benefit enormously from proper training. At this time there were no Catholic training colleges in Ireland, and there were approximately 7,000 untrained teachers in Irish schools. Bernie Joyce notes:

> When two Catholic training colleges were established in 1883, the Catholic sisters could not avail of them, because under their vows taken on profession [attendance] would be a violation of such.[14]

The Catholic Sisters were at a distinct disadvantage, in comparison with their lay contemporaries, who were able to avail of the training provided. Agnes started a campaign to remedy this situation. In 1910 she was instrumental in establishing a teacher training college in Milltown, County Dublin, for the Sisters of her own order. In 1913 the Milltown training college gained recognition from the National Board of Education. Agnes pushed on, and negotiated for the establishment of summer schools in the Irish Catholic training colleges to accommodate Sisters from other orders who were without access to training. In a letter to Archbishop William Walsh, Agnes outlined the case for the summer schools:

> When the Episcopal body met last June at Maynooth our ecclesiastical superior, Most Rev. Dr. Walsh brought under their notice St. Mary's Training College at Milltown, where our Mother General gives a two year's [*sic*] course to the Sisters employed in our Convent National schools. The Bishops formed a committee in June to draft a similar scheme for the benefit of other Convents ... I take the liberty of drawing your attention to the fact that there are many Convents in Ireland who would gladly send their School Sisters for a two year's [*sic*] course of training, but their staff being limited makes it impossible. There are hundreds of Nuns, who have been employed for many years in the Primary Schools, who would derive great benefit from a 'Summer School' if they could get a month's training in July, during the long vacation when the three Training Colleges of Carysfort, Belfast and Limerick are vacant. These Colleges are splendidly equipped and have every accommodation for each to board and lodge 100 Nuns. The Authorities could easily select an efficient staff of teachers, who would put them through the teaching of the National School Programme ... I have heard various Inspectors say with regret that Nuns will be forced

in the near future to take back seats unless some Scheme is adopted which will get them a recognition of competence to conduct and teach Schools with full educational efficiency … [W]hen Sisters would return to their respective Convents, they could during the following year impart to other members of their communities the information they had received. Seeing the many advantages our Sisters have derived since Mother General started her Training College is my apology for bringing this important matter under your notice.[15]

There was a general belief among the clergy and laity of Ireland, that the foundress of the Irish Sisters of Charity, Mary Aikenhead, by the sanctity of her life and the charity of her labours, had merited the honours of beatification and canonisation.[16] On her death, in July 1858, Dr Paul Cullen, Archbishop of Dublin, remarked, 'Who ever did more for religion than she?'[17] Agnes had been hopeful for some time that a procedure for the beatification of Mary Aikenhead might soon be commenced. On 22 July 1908, the fiftieth anniversary of Mary Aikenhead's death was commemorated at Milltown. Bishop McCormack preached on the occasion and compared Mary Aikenhead to St Camillus and St Vincent de Paul. He referred to her 'letters replete with some of the best lessons in ascetic theology'.[18]

Shortly after this, Agnes received a letter from Mother Gertrude Davis, Superioress in St Mary's Convent, Parramatta, a suburb of Sydney, Australia, expressing the hope that the process for Mary Aikenhead's beatification would soon be undertaken. In her reply Agnes asked Mother Gertrude to seek the intervention of Cardinal Moran, nephew of Cardinal Cullen. This great churchman must have heard his uncle speak in praise of Mary Aikenhead. Moreover Cardinal Moran had been a chaplain in Mountjoy Street convent, and had been nursed through a serious illness by the Sisters of Charity. It appeared that Agnes's request had been successful when a letter arrived on 20 December 1909 from Cardinal Moran to the Mother General in Milltown:

> There is something quite miraculous in her [Mary Aikenhead's] whole career. The hand of Providence is seen at every step in the wondrous ways by which she was prepared for the arduous task that awaited her ... I am confident that Mary Aikenhead was a great Saint.[19]

But the informative process had to be taken on by an Irish bishop and it would be a lengthy and arduous task. Gildea tells us:

> On 5th May, 1911, Monsignor Don Descuffi assured Agnes of success, if Archbishop Walsh of Dublin or some Irish Bishop would undertake the work ... [H]owever, a diocesan court had to introduce the cause. The difficulty of finding a Bishop willing to accept the responsibility of Mary Aikenhead's cause is easily understood. The Sisters of Charity had communities only in five Irish dioceses. Their Foundress was buried in Dublin, their Novitiate and Mother House was in Dublin. The Postulator strongly favoured the Dublin diocesan court. But Archbishop Walsh of Dublin was not available, and neither was Dr Sheehan, Bishop of Waterford when approached. Weary months of waiting passed. Hopes and fears alternated in the heart of Agnes and the Sisters of Charity. Then came the news that Dr. Morrisroe [from Charlestown, County Mayo, only a few miles from Foxford] was selected by the Pope as Bishop of the Diocese of Achonry, where three convents of the Sisters of Charity were situated. One first-class and several second-class witnesses for the cause were living in the Diocese.[20]

This surely must have seemed to Agnes to be the hand of Providence working again in her favour. When the newly consecrated bishop visited Foxford convent, Agnes asked, 'Will your Lordship act as Judge?'

> For a few minutes the young prelate was silent. The nun's heart was beating fast, and her lips moved in silent prayer. The answer put an end to many disappointments and anxieties. 'Yes,' said His Lordship, 'in the name of God I will take up the cause.'[21]

Dr Morrisroe,
Bishop of Achonry.

A decree was issued by Bishop Donnelly V.G. (in the absence of Archbishop Walsh), in the Archdiocese of Dublin. A copy of the decree was sent to the bishops of the dioceses where Mother Mary Aikenhead had made foundations. It was to be affixed to church doors from 1 to 30 September 1912 (see Appendix 2).

> In 1911 Agnes undertook the job of Secretary. This entailed a huge amount of work for her. She worked consistently and

tirelessly. A huge volume of correspondence passed between the Foxford and Roman secretaries. The Postulator in Rome, Monsignor Carinci, had drawn up 256 articles in connection with the life and virtues of Mary Aikenhead.[22]

In 1918 the writings of Mary Aikenhead were examined and approved in Rome and this was a cause of great joy for Agnes and her community. Three years later there was cause for further hope, when:

> In 1921 Pope Benedict XV signed the Decree for the Introduction of the Cause of Beatification of the Servant of God, Mary Aikenhead. Of its subject the Decree tells of the 'fame of her holiness of Life', and later recalls that the 'sacred obsequies of Mary Aikenhead were, for their solemnity and the concourse of people, compared by eyewitnesses to the famous funeral of Daniel O'Connell'.[23]

Circumstances were to get in the way of the work, however. The process was not as straightforward as imagined. Political upheavals in Ireland and two world wars, were factors that delayed the process. Moreover 1934 brought about a change in the process:

> It was decided in Rome that the Cause must be examined by the new Historical Commission set up by Pope Pius XI in 1930 for those Causes which were deficient in evidence from first class witnesses. This was the case with Mary Aikenhead's Cause because it was not taken up until 53 years after her death. Consequently there were very few first class witnesses. So her Cause was now required to go to this new Commission and fulfil the requirements stipulated.

This was very disappointing for the promoters of the Cause in Ireland and Australia, because effectively work on the Cause had to begin again.[24]

Sadly Agnes did not live to see the cause of Mary Aikenhead brought to fruition, as she passed away before it could be fulfilled. In 1958 the Irish government issued a stamp to commemorate her life's work. The quest has continued down through the years and a number of people have been involved in the process, including Sister Marie Bernadette O'Leary, current archivist of the Irish Sisters of Charity repository in Sandymount, Dublin. A new postulator, Monsignor Ciaran O'Carroll, was appointed in 2013, with Sister Josephine McDonald as vice-postulator.[25]

The bicentenary of the foundation of the Irish Sisters of Charity is in 2015, so it may be that Mary Aikenhead will be declared venerable to coincide with this anniversary. Sister Marie Bernadette O'Leary said:

> Next year is a significant one for our order; it being its bi-
> centenary. It is hoped that Mary Aikenhead may be declared
> venerable by the Holy Father. The Cause of Mary Aikenhead has
> been passed by the historical and theological commission. The
> road to canonisation is indeed a lengthy and rigorous process.[26]

Another one of Agnes's greatest campaigns seems to be on the road to completion.

Agnes also played a key role in the case of Mary Charles Walker, who was intent on serving as a missionary in Calabar. Margaret Mary Angela Walker, one of six children, was born to upper-middle-class English parents in Brighton, England, in 1881. In 1891 her mother died and she was sent to Mayfield School, in East Sussex, once the holiday retreat of the Archbishops of Canterbury.

It would appear that her admission to the Sisters of Charity came at the influence of Fr Peter Gallwey, former provincial of the Irish Jesuits, who was a frequent visitor to the school and was much sought after as a retreat master and spiritual director. She entered as a Sister of Charity in Mount St Anne's, Milltown, Co. Dublin on 21 November 1901. She was professed on 26 May, 1904 and took the name of Sr Mary Charles.[27]

*Mary Charles Walker
(Sister Magdalen).*

Sister Mary Charles' first assignment was at the convent primary school at Basin Lane, James's Street, Dublin, a poor area of the city. In 1912 she was transferred to St Vincent's convent school in Cork, and three years later she was transferred to Foxford convent, where over the next five to six years Agnes would become her closest confidante.

> It is probable that the basis for this friendship came from the similar family backgrounds, and sympathies that both shared before entering religion, and from the common bond that united them in the years in Foxford, the call of the foreign missions.[28]

In August 1920 Sister Mary Charles was transferred to Ravenswell Convent in Bray, County Wicklow. Cooke indicates that:

> It was a wrench for her to leave Foxford where she had made

her closest friend in the congregation. She taught in the school and her spare time was occupied in preparing a small booklet on the work of the congregation entitled *Caritas Christi Urget Nos*. It breathes her love and regard for the congregation and this at a time when she was facing the decision that she might well have to sever her links with it if her desire to work on the missions was to be effected.[29]

Here is a summation of Sister Mary Charles Walker by one of her fellow members of the Foxford congregation:

> Shortly afterwards I went to Foxford and found that all were unanimous in agreeing that she was, what now-a-days would be described as a dedicated religious, silent and a strict observer of Rule. Any adverse criticism was that she was not a good mixer, she did not seem to have contributed much to their recreations. Hers was a serious mind, devoted to her school work, to the salvation of souls, and to contemplative prayer ... An ascetic, austere religious, very courteous, deeply silent. She gave me the impression that she prized belonging to our congregation very highly.[30]

The idea of a mission of the Sisters of Charity in Nigeria came at the invitation of Bishop Joseph Shanahan. Shanahan was born on 6 June 1871 in Glankeen, County Tipperary. On 22 April 1900 he was ordained a priest in Blackrock College and he served as dean of the boarding school in Rockwell. In 1902 he was appointed to the Mission of Southern Nigeria and left Ireland on 9 October of that year on his first missionary journey. On 27 September 1905 Fr Shanahan was appointed Prefect Apostolic of Lower Niger. On 6 June 1920, at Maynooth College, he was ordained Bishop of Southern Nigeria.[31]

Shanahan's first assignment was to help Fr Léon Lejeune in making bricks to build the first proper mission house in Onitsha. He soon learned that the future of the mission depended mainly on the use of schools to evangelise the parents through their children. Mindful all along of the necessity to provide a good Christian education for women, Bishop Shanahan tried for years to find a missionary society especially devoted to that ministry.

Bishop Joseph Shanahan.

Shanahan expresses this wish in a letter to his Superior General on 18 July 1914. He hoped, he said, that three Sisters of Charity would be made available. At a meeting with Mother Agnes Gertrude Chamberlain, the Mother General, he proposed that the convent at Onitsha would be made available to the Sisters and that he would defray all expenses involved. He hoped that she would make an inspection tour to Nigeria before a final decision was made.

On 27 August 1914 the superiors of all houses of the congregation received a letter from Mother Agnes Gertrude, outlining Bishop Shanahan's proposals regarding the establishment of the mission. This letter, as well as some notes that outlined the type of person suitable for the vicariate, was read publicly to the community in each house:

> There is grand work to be done for souls in Nigeria, and no doubt there would be many consolations. At the same time it is well for all to know that the climate is one of the worst in the world; the language is another difficulty. Any person going there should be of a very generous nature, and prepared to bear

many hardships cheerfully, and to lead a life altogether different to what we are accustomed to in this country. Now I must ask all to be prudent in what they say about the project, as too much talk is very likely to do more harm than good ... and I would recommend those who are interested in the work to try by exact observance of Rule to become possessed of those virtues stated by the Prefect Apostolic to be necessary fall missionaries, otherwise they will never be fit subjects for so great a mission ...

Missionary sisters should be physically strong ... [A] youthful and vigorous constitution stands the best chance. Persons over forty years of age would experience a certain difficulty in becoming adapted to the strange surroundings and conditions ... I know several priests who went out to Africa when they were well over forty; they lived for many years and did splendid work. All missionaries, there is no exception, must be strict observers of the Rule of their Orders; they must have a real sensible zeal for the salvation of souls and be animated by high supernatural motives. They should be generous, filled with the spirit of self-sacrifice, humble and obedient and of a cheerful disposition. The sisters will have to do missionary work of the first order; to co-operate directly in the salvation of souls.

There is nobody doing the same work that they will have to do; if they don't come out to do it, forever it shall remain undone. There are numbers of people waiting for somebody to teach them catechism; there are schools, sodalities, and sick people of every age and description to be looked after ... A cer-tificated elementary teacher with a fully qualified nurse would be invaluable. There must be no concealing of the fact that at first, life in the tropics is not pleasant. The climate is trying, the devil is not idle, his hatred makes him redouble his efforts and his attacks on the missioners, because they are invading his kingdom. Then there are days when one feels feverish and bilious. On such days, community life is meritorious but not agreeable. Africa brings out and shows up the weak points in one's character and temper. It is humiliating for the missionary to have to acknowledge the presence of so many weak points in his spiritual fortress. Humility is the only remedy. Far above the beauties of nature are the daily miracles wrought in human souls by the grace of God. It is the missioner's happy lot, day after day, to open the gates of heaven; to open the heart of man and to allow heaven and earth, God and His creature to meet the poor here before meeting for ever in heaven.[32]

This missive was much debated, and a number of issues emerged. Firstly, a mission foundation could only be countenanced with the permission of the congregation's ecclesiastical superior, Archbishop William Walsh of Dublin. He was not in favour of a mission undertaking. Secondly, a mission foundation would require certain changes in the constitutions of the congregation. Even if these were overcome, the outbreak of the First World War pre-empted any possible reconnaissance of the mission. It is also likely that another consideration influenced discussions. In 1818 Mother Mary Aikenhead had sent Sisters to Australia. After a short time it became clear that the ecclesiastical superior in Sydney had totally different views on the role of the Sisters from those of Mother Mary Aikenhead. It was not possible to govern the Australian convent from Dublin, and a separate congregation was formed in 1842. This raised the problem of the direction of a centralised congregation of convents in distant parts. On 25 April 1915 Mother Agnes Gertrude informed Shanahan of her decision:

You may remember calling here, last year, in reference to a convent of Sisters being founded in Nigeria. At that time, I promised, if I got the approval of our Ecclesiastical superior, the Archbishop of Dublin, to accept your invitation to go, with two of ours, to see the place where the establishment was to be made; I also promised to have prayers offered that we might know the Will of God regarding the proposed foundation. I now wish to let you know that my term of office as Superior General will expire on the 12th of next month, so the matter is completely at an end, as far as I am concerned.[33]

Mother Agnes Gertrude was in fact re-elected as Mother General, and the question of a mission in Nigeria was far from over in the congregation. Bishop Shanahan was bitterly disappointed. His disappointment was exacerbated by the withdrawal from the mission of the Sisters of St Joseph of Cluny in 1919. In September 1919 he decided to reopen negotiations with the Sisters of Charity. The request was channelled through the Rectress at Mount Merrion, Sister Joseph Conception Vavasour. She took up the question once more with the Mother General, who in turn advised her to consult Agnes in Foxford. Agnes replied as follows:

If you get a clear understanding in writing from all parties concerned and duly signed it ought to clear away many stumbling blocks. I would suggest your making out two lists of names (i) of the honorary members who would promise to pray for the success of the Nigerian mission and give any help in their power. (ii) A list of twelve names of practical earnest workers, who have spent much time in prayer and mature consideration and believe that they have got a special call for the Nigerian Mission and feel perfectly indifferent to failure or success, good or bad health, provided they are allowed to start for Nigeria when Mgr Shanahan returns there. On that list I would ask you to include your own name for your heart is set on making the trail, also that of Sr M. Charles Walker, who has been a member of this community for the last four years. She seems to have all the qualifications which ought to make her a success as a successful teacher in the Nigerian schools. Though I never lived with Sr T. Magdalen Harold Barry, the time she spent in schools, as mistress of penitents and as Rectress, ought to make her a useful subject. You would require two sisters that have got practical hospital training, and one that would make a suitable ministress and general factotum, amiable and ready and willing to help in all difficulties. Avoid a 'wet blanket' or a 'crank.' They are a scourge in a small community where kindred spirits are real blessings.[34]

A number of Sisters expressed their desire to volunteer for the missions. Among the Foxford community was Sister Stanislaus Cullen, a niece of Archbishop Cullen, who was one of the most prominent members of the Catholic clergy in Ireland, and Mary Charles Walker. While the matter was being discussed, Shanahan visited Agnes at Foxford in 1919. Cooke states that her reaction to him was surprising and unexpected, all the more so in view of her subsequent friendship and support.[35] Agnes in her notes recalled:

> Mgr Shanahan called here and I promised to do what I could to promote the Foreign Missions but was prejudiced against himself personally – feeling that he had treated the two nuns in Calabar (Sisters of St. Joseph of Cluny) in a very drastic manner and fearing that he would be too autocratic in his dealing with our Sister, who might be at his mercy, so far from our Mother General.[36]

It was during this visit that Sister Mary Charles Walker was introduced to Shanahan. She expressed the hope that she would be selected for Nigeria and he expressed satisfaction at her suitability for mission work, 'especially for his school in Calabar'. However, while Agnes had been dubious in her mind about Shanahan, she had since 1915 'made various inquiries which disabused my former prejudices' and now wholeheartedly supported the venture.[37] Agnes pushed for the cause in correspondence with the Mother General, who in turn wrote to Agnes:

> I have no objections to Foreign Missions but would like to see them started by a sensible woman on whose judgement I could rely. If the Archbishop asked me now what I thought I would have to say that from my point of view the present agitation was on a bad foundation and he would have to give me a decided command on the matter.[38]

However, she allowed the question of the mission to be re-opened and appointed a committee of Sisters to study the proposal submitted by Bishop Shanahan. On 24 October 1919, Mother Agnes Joseph Smyth informed Shanahan on behalf of the Mother General that she was unable to accept his invitation at the present time. Another disappointment for Shanahan, but despite this Agnes persisted in her campaign for the mission. The way in which she furthered it revolved around the Cause for the beatification of Mother Mary Aikenhead. When the decree for this was signed by the Pope, Agnes decided that the congregation should show its joy through a magnificent gesture, which she thought should take the form of the mission in Nigeria.

The general assembly of the order was meeting in Dublin in May 1920, and she had a motion included on the agenda, urging the meeting to accept Shanahan's offer and to send six Sisters to Nigeria before 1 November. The debate was heated and many expressed the view that the needs of Ireland and England must come before the needs of Africa. The motion was rejected by seventy votes to seven.

Agnes had to admit defeat, saying, 'Nigeria is quite off and definitely dead.'[39] However, despite the pressures of her work, she made time to communicate with Shanahan and even send him gifts. He expressed his gratitude in a letter:

> I have to thank you for your letter of the 21 January enclosing harps and shamrock for St Patrick's Day, [and] picture postcards of your beautiful new convent chapel, recently consecrated ... Foxford recalls to my mind some of the happiest hours of my life. We will talk once more about Nigeria and the prospects of the realization of the greatest dream of your apostolic life – that lies no longer within me but with holy providence, as I will explain when we meet. I only wish I had your daring trust in God and in what God expects from each of his children.[40]

Sister Mary Charles Walker decided she wanted to go to Nigeria on her own. The Sisters of Charity were aghast, as were canon lawyers and, most of all, the Archbishop of Dublin, Dr Edward Byrne. Sister Mary Charles was told that nobody except the Pope could grant her permission to leave her community in such circumstances. She said that she would be quite happy to ask the Pope. In 1922 the Mother General transferred Mary Charles Walker to the Sisters of Charity convent in Chiswick, London, to be near her dying father. Another reason for her transfer was that she would be under the jurisdiction of Cardinal Bourne, with whom Shanahan had discussed her case, and who was likely to be more sympathetic than Archbishop Byrne.

Her application had gone to Rome at this stage, and Cardinal Bourne gave her his full support. In April 1923 Shanahan heard that permission for her to travel to Nigeria was granted. In June the final document arrived in London. Shanahan wrote to Mary Martin, foundress of the Medical Missionaries of Mary:

> Good news, Sr Charles is free. She, while remaining a religious, is permitted to live outside her convent, the first evident sign that her work, the foundation of missionary society of Sisters, has the approval of God.[41]

Mary Martin had met Shanahan on 29 April 1920. In 1921 she had sailed for Nigeria at Shanahan's request. She trained as a nurse and midwife and worked as a lay missionary in Calabar.

> Religious women were not allowed to practice medicine. It was only in February 1936 that the decree *Constans ac Sedula*, was published permitting women religious to practice all branches of medicine, including obstetrics and surgery.[42]

Bishop Shanahan organised travel arrangements for Sister Mary Charles, and decided that, in view of the fact that she was now attached to the Vicariate of Southern Nigeria rather than the Sisters of Charity, she should take a new religious name. She chose the name Magdalen in memory of a recently dead sister, and during her time in Nigeria was known as Sister Magdalen. Mary Charles Walker arrived in Nigeria in September 1923 taking charge of the only girls' school in the vicariate:

> Sister Mary Charles proved to be an outstanding educator and was instrumental not only in the reorganization and setting up of numerous schools, but also in the creation of an indigenous

religious congregation – The Congregation of the Handmaids of the Holy Child Jesus (HHCH) in 1931.[43]

Agnes was a constant support in the life of Mary Charles Walker, as a friend, adviser and practical helper:

> Agnes kept Mary Charles Walker supplied with books for the senior classes and toys and Montessori equipment for the juniors. In addition she sent out the latest books on religion and education for Mary Charles's own use, and the convent gradually built up a small but well-chosen library. Many of the priests would call on her when in Calabar and borrow the latest Chesterton or Belloc – they did not always remember to bring them back.[44]

The following illustrates the constant support Agnes offered to Mary Charles Walker and that her cause was always close to Agnes's heart:

> Your friends around here have not forgotten you, and are very anxious to help you to take in a few more girls that are in danger ... Sr. M. Assissium had her musical entertainment in the Music School on 5th Jan. After expenses were cleared M. Rectress said in her opinion you were the greatest pity being so far away without any help, and the work so praiseworthy your good Bishop deserves help. We are sending £45 from entertainment and my five separate, so this makes a total of £50. So put down your 1st foundation stone under the invocation of Divine Providence, that providence that provides us with all natural & supernatural gifts. It has astounded everyone to get this out of a small little village ... [T]he object appealed to all, and you were so well known and loved by children and teachers.[45]

Throughout the 1920s Agnes continued to press for members of her order to establish a congregation in Nigeria. It became clear that Bishop Shanahan would not request the order to establish a congregation in his diocese again. The Mother General, Mother Agnes Gertrude Chamberlain, was not enthusiastic either. It became clear to Mary Charles Walker at this stage that Agnes's campaign was proving futile. She wrote to Agnes:

> I am sure God will give a Foreign Mission to the Sisters of Charity. But the Bishop does not wish me to take part in the matter in any way. Also we beg that you will not show my letters to anyone outside the [Foxford] community, and that you will not write about me to anyone in Rome or in places of authority. As a Sister of Charity, both Mother General and other authorities wish me to be looked upon as extinct. This was the cause of my change of name – not a compliment to Magdalen. I have marked some passages in your letter to Mgr Descuffe where the information is mistaken. I am afraid that if my letters are shown or extracts made of them, the Bishop will not wish me to write to Ireland anymore. Mary Aikenhead will get sisters to the Foreign Missions in her own way. We think it more likely that they will go to China especially now that the Jesuits are going.[46]

At this stage Mary Charles Walker knew that as long as Bishop Shanahan was Superior, the mission that she and Agnes desired would never come to fruition. In a letter to Agnes, she wrote:

> If my conscience does not allow me to make any effort to bring about what you and I desire, I am not inactive in prayer, nor also when opportunity offers itself with my immediate superior. But I think that you cannot expect the Bishop to ask again after being so often refused.[47]

However, Agnes never lost hope in the belief that a mission would be established in Nigeria. In one letter to Mary Charles Walker, she writes:

> I spoke to Fr Finlay freely about Nigeria and its prospects. He told me that the Irish Jesuits are now going to have a Foreign Mission but have not as yet come to a decision as to where it will be. I told him of the strong wish I had that Jesuits might go to Nigeria. He mentioned that wherever they went their portion should be completely and distinctly assigned to themselves as they got their experience in England that anything else would not suit. Their Fathers had been given Parishes to take charge of, and having done so, erected Churches, Colleges, Schools etc., and after the death of the bishop who brought them there, one of his successors removed them elsewhere! It taught them a sad and salutary lesson never to be caught again by the successors of those who bring them to a mission. This affords ample scope for deep meditation and just gives you a mere outline of what can be done if your good Bishop thinks well of it. If they got a tract of land with say 2,000,000 pagans to work out as best they could with schools, a college and seminary to train future native priests, it ought to be a great help to Dr. Shanahan. But Father Finlay told me that the first step would be to apply to the General of the Jesuits in Rome asking for a branch of the Irish Province. This is imperative and would not be successful otherwise. Then it would be easy to negotiate with the Provincial in Ireland and with Propaganda.[48]

Agnes decided at this point to withdraw from the campaign, and leave the establishment of a mission to her Order. Nearer to home, it was through Agnes's intervention that other Orders of nuns arrived in Mayo:

The Sisters effected a spiritual renewal not only in Foxford but in the Diocese of Achonry as a whole. It was through the influence of Arsenius that the Sisters of St. Louis established their convent in Kiltimagh. When the Sisters of Mercy were having difficulties in finding a suitable superior for their convent at Swinford, in the early 1890s, it was Arsenius who helped resolve the crisis and introduced Mother Evangelista McCarthy to the community. It was on the basis of this community's strength that two new foundations of Mercy sisters were established at Collooney and Ballymote (Co. Sligo), two towns which had been the object of Arsenius's concern years earlier. She was also responsible for the introduction of the Franciscan Brothers to Foxford in 1925.[49]

On 5 June 1855, Sisters Aloysius Martyn and De Sales Coppinger had come from the Convent of Mercy in Tuam to start a community of Sisters of Mercy in Swinford, County Mayo. A newly built convent was ready for them. A primary school, under the National Education Board, opened in 1856 and in 1906 a secondary school was established. By 1912 this included a boarding school. In 1925 St Anne's Public Laundry was established to give employment locally.

> Agnes was to the forefront again as it was she who trained Mother M. Columbanus Flatley on the keeping of accounts and general administration of the laundry.[50]

Agnes proved to be a true and fearless campaigner in what she believed was good for the community. She wanted just and proper treatment to be accorded to each person, regardless of creed, colour or culture.

Agnes and the Politics of the Time

⤙⤚

THE UPCOMING ELECTION of July 1892 was much talked about by many parties. The Irish Parliamentary Party was split at this time, with the majority of its MPs, the Anti-Parnellites, supporting John Dillon, while Parnell's followers supported John Redmond, leader of the Home Rule party.

Demonstrations and fighting among party loyals were commonplace, and in Foxford one such incident was to have repercussions at the woollen mill, which had been in existence a mere three months. A Parnellite demonstration took place in the town, and the parish priest, Fr Michael O'Donnell, was heckled as he passed by. Among the demonstrators were some of the employees of the mill. The priests called to the convent and demanded that six of the workers be dismissed. The first was the carpenter, John O'Donnell, then Mary Henehan, a teacher in the school, and four other girls, all belonging to families that supported Parnell. Fr Michael O'Donnell informed Agnes that he had been in contact with Bishop Lyster and was acting on his advice. Agnes suspended the six workers temporarily, but refused to be intimidated, saying that the mill was being made a 'party machine, a reward for good nationalists; no others need apply'. In a letter to the bishop she stated:

I felt bound to make a firm stand and I refused emphatically to agree to their demand. We Sisters of Charity have no politics … I came here to help the poor, non-sectarian, and non-political. So long as they require my help they shall have it and I will submit to no interference. We are not Sisters of Mercy under local authority. I am under that of my Superior General and recognise no other. If we are not allowed to do the work we came for, then, we go … I am ready to close down the mill, to leave on short notice and leave you the care of your own poor, the responsibility is with you.[1]

A week later the curate informed Agnes that her school would be placed under interdict if the parties involved did not proffer an apology. Agnes as ever maintained her calm demeanour:

I repeated what I had said a week ago and added that I considered that my community was being badly treated. Our schools and grounds were private property and I would allow no action to be taken there that savoured of politics.[2]

However, she did acknowledge that the employees had been less than gracious to Fr O'Donnell and that an apology would be forthcoming. She spoke to the parties involved:

I told them I would go with them next day and before the congregation after last Mass I would speak for them. It was a vital moment, the life or death of our work in Foxford depended on it. I insisted that the two priests should come to the church door, and there I made my first and last public speech and read the apology I had written out for them as follows. We have come to express our regret that any disrespect has been shown by us or anyone belonging to us to any of the priests as the

ministers of God and our holy religion and humbly beg of
you, Father O'Donnell, as our parish priest, and of you, Father
Callaghan as curate, to allow the Reverend Mother to take us
back into her employment which she promised to do as soon as
we make this act of reparation for what has occurred.[3]

Mary Henehan was the only one who was not excused, the parish priest explaining that there had been bad blood between
himself and her father for some time. Fr Denis O'Hara intervened and told the family to leave Mary's case in Agnes's hands.
Fr O'Donnell informed Agnes that the Henehans should not
be allowed into the convent. Agnes told him plainly that the
convent doors would be open to every waif and stray, that it was
a universal refuge for all.

> Fr Callaghan had visited the schools previously and had urged
> the Sisters to 'take decisive action' to get some of the parents of
> the children to change their political leanings.[4]

Agnes did not agree with this policy. The parish priest threatened
to leave the Sisters without Mass.

Agnes wrote to Bishop Lyster, whom she said 'so injudiciously
acceded to the priests demand' of placing the school under
interdict.[5] Bishop Lyster visited Foxford a month later and after
a lengthy process the case was resolved. Agnes recorded the
event in her memoirs:

> God arose and scattered his enemies and our little barque
> once again weathered a violent storm, which had threatened
> to submerge our work, and leave the banks of the Moy as
> destitute as they had formerly been. And why? Because men
> allowed their political feelings to overflow and because a couple

of opponents boohed, and their little girls thought they should do what their dadas did![6]

The relationship between the bishop and Agnes seemed to remain strained for the rest of his life. On one occasion he visited the convent to inspect the mill's accounts. She regarded this as somewhat beyond his remit. The next time the accounts were audited, Agnes sent a Sister over to the bishop's residence with an abstract of the accounts, sufficiently complex to prevent enlightenment, and with strict orders that she have them home with her again that evening. When Dr Lyster died in 1911, he endowed each convent in the diocese, including two other foundations of the Irish Sisters of Charity, but omitted Foxford.[7]

Politics raised its head on a number of occasions during Agnes's lifetime, and she had to deal with many controversial issues. She and her community witnessed the Great War of 1914–18, the Easter Rising of 1916, the War of Independence from 1919–21 and the Irish Civil War from 1922–23.

The outbreak of the war in 1914 brought a new difficulty. The British government introduced strict rules on the sale and purchase of wool.

> Frank Sherry, the Manager, became so alarmed after a slump in sales that he was forced to suggest to Agnes that she should put the employees on half-time. Mother Rectress did not take long to reply. They are Providence Mills, and the Sisters will have to go before we stop the poor people from earning a living; let them make blankets if they have nothing to do, and by degrees we will get rid of them. The workers started to produce the blankets, until nothing else could be seen upstairs or downstairs.[8]

Again, it appears that Providence was on Agnes's side. On 14
September 1916:

> A wire came in from the War Office to know if they could get
> 2,000 blankets before the end of the month. To complete this
> order within the time would have been impossible, were it not
> that we had 15,000 in stock thanks to the unfailing faith in
> Divine Providence shown in this emergency.[9]

Gregory and Paseta refer to this acquisition of blankets for the
army:

> The expanding army, conscripted in Britain from May 1916, had
> to be supplied. A slow build up of War Office contracts arrived
> for Irish firms, principally textile and clothing companies. By
> 1917 Irish woollen mills were turning out blankets throughout
> the country. Woollen mills in Midleton, Glenties, Foxford,
> Tralee, Ballygawley, Dripsey, Galway, Beaufort, Lisbellaw,
> Castlederg, Kilmeaden and Crumlin, Co. Antrim were working
> on War Office contracts.[10]

The War of Independence brought its own anguish. This was
a guerrilla war mounted by the Irish Republican Army (IRA)
against the British government and its forces in Ireland. It
began on 21 January 1919, following Dáil Éireann's declaration
of independence earlier that same day. Both sides agreed to a
ceasefire on 11 July 1921. The Civil War broke out on 28 June
1922 and continued until 24 May 1923:

> The conflict waged between two opposing groups of Irish
> nationalists, over the Anglo-Irish Treaty. One group, the Free-
> Staters, or the pro-treaty supporters, favoured it, while the

Republican opposition, the IRA, saw it as a betrayal of the Irish Republic. The Republic was established during the War of Independence, and many of those who fought in the conflict had been members of the Irish Republican Army during that war. The conflict saw brother fight against brother and left Irish society divided and embittered for generations.[11]

During the War of Independence, in September 1920, Agnes wrote to Sir Horace Plunkett telling him of her fear of an attack on the woollen mills by the crown forces. Plunkett contacted Dublin Castle, where the British administration was based:

> I told those I met the romantic story of your wonderful enterprise and they said that it seemed inconceivable that anybody under any circumstances whatsoever would do it harm.[12]

Throughout the War of Independence the RIC was continually targeted, as they were perceived as being the principal enemy of the people. Barracks where police were stationed were regularly attacked and often burned down. In the early hours of 24 May 1921, the inhabitants of Foxford awoke to the sound of gunfire from the RIC barracks. The attack was carried out by a small group of IRA Volunteers and in itself was quite harmless. In its official report, published in the national newspapers the next day, Dublin Castle reported:

> at 3 a.m. yesterday, Foxford (Mayo) barracks were attacked by a number of men armed with rifles and bombs. The attack was beaten off at 4 a.m. There were no casualties.[13]

The incident would have passed off almost unnoticed, but for the extreme response of the crown forces stationed at Swinford. On

Friday 27 May, army personnel from Swinford arrived in Foxford and proceeded to round up a number of young men. They brought five to Swinford and left another four in Foxford barracks.

> Later that night, two of the prisoners were taken from Swinford station out onto the public road, where they were met by three officers. They were slashed with crop whips, and marched to a nearby river, where they were stripped, painted in green, white and yellow, before being thrown head first into the water. The four men in Foxford barracks were taken by officers and marched through the town to the bridge, where they were flogged with whips. The officers told them if they attempted to run they would be shot.[14]

One of these men, John (Seán) Higgins, was an employee at the woollen mill in the town. Agnes was furious at the treatment meted out to the men and she chose to act. She sent a cutting report to General Neville Macready, outlining in graphic detail the terrible ordeal that the men had endured at the hands of the crown forces. Six months later, on 6 November 1921, the victims applied to Swinford Quarter Sessions for compensation for the injuries they sustained in the attack. The *Western People* carried a report on the case:

> The abominable indignities to which the claimants had been subjected were of so revolting a nature that the Judge, in denouncing them, said that they reflected the gravest discredit and called for the gravest censure on the persons guilty of them.[15]

Seán Higgins later met his fate during the Civil War. On 16 September 1922 Higgins and Captain Tom Healy, both members of the National Army, were killed in a fierce battle at Glenamoy, County Mayo, both shot by the anti-Treaty IRA. James Laffey describes the scene at Foxford railway station:

> Two days later hundreds of townspeople gathered at Foxford railway station to meet the train that had conveyed their tri-coloured draped coffins from Ballina. On the following morning, a huge procession, headed by the Foxford Brass and Reed Band, accompanied the funeral cortege to the recently opened cemetery at Craggagh, where the two young men were laid to rest in an area known as the Patriot's Plot.[16]

Captain Tom Healy and John (Seán) Higgins.

Higgins was not the only employee of the mill who was directly affected by the War of Independence. Frank Sherry wrote in his notes about a search of his home by the Black and Tans, who were ruthless and unsympathetic by his account:

> At a later date we had a visit from two Black and Tans who entered my house at 7 a.m. one day and searched every inch of it and gave particular attention to the papers in my desk: it was quite a formidable task but availed them nothing. If they hoped for some seditious document or something that would connect us with the IRA activities they were disappointed. I had no

politics; I had a job to do and gave all my attention to it because it seemed to me worth doing well.[17]

He continues:

I could see in the lives and homes of the people the reflection of what the coming of Providence Mills meant to the district. Ceaseless work and ceaseless care were necessary to keep that effort going, especially in such unquiet times, and I thought I was not serving my country too badly if I did my ordinary day's work. I could look back to the potatoes and Indian meal diet of the people in earlier days and contrast it with the still modest but more varied table that wage earning had made possible. I could in quiet moments recapture the smell of the mud cabins where the pig and poultry dwelt with the poor family, not because the poor approved of that arrangement but because they had no better way and were too harassed, sick and sad to plan better ways. I could remember the manure heaps where the vegetable gardens are now. I had gone into the homes where a sick man or woman lay on hay or even rushes on the floor.[18]

The government decided to prohibit the Foxford Fair on 15 May 1921, causing considerable hardship to farmers who could not sell their cattle. Agnes wrote to District Inspector McGarry in Swinford, pleading with him to allow the holding of the June fair. She also accused the police of inflicting unnecessary hardship on the people of Foxford by imposing a curfew after 6 p.m:

Curfew regulations and the prohibition of the use of bicycles have placed most unjust hardships on the poor unfortunate workers here. Heretofore, the workers could cycle to their homes for their meals, and after working in the mill could do nearly a half-day's work on their bog, saving turf, and in their little plots gardening and farming, and the factory girls used to enjoy a good long walk in the dusk of the twilight after a hard day's work. All this is now absolutely impossible. For the last week not a drop of rain fell – which is very unusual in Foxford and it is heartrending to see turf badly in need of turning in the bogs and the poor people not able to attend to it. This is the only way they have of putting in a supply of fuel for the winter months. In the interests of common humanity – not to speak of either justice or charity – both these regulations, involving so much hardship, ought to be removed.[19]

There was little McGarry could do about the curfew, and he admitted to Agnes that he had not been consulted about it. Agnes acknowledged that it put him in an awkward position, as he had been on friendly terms with the locals.[20] A few days later Agnes received a visit from a British officer. In his notes Frank Sherry recounted:

I remember the day in her own office that I stood by her side as manager, as a tall suave officer of the English army called on some pertinent business. The superior was old then, the small frame bent and feeble. The officer saw before him an old and probably timid nun, 'don't be afraid Mother' he encouraged her as he entered – 'young man' she said, 'I am afraid of nothing but sin' – the military gentleman was rendered speechless.[21]

In a letter to Horace Plunkett, Agnes enclosed a report of the atrocities committed there by the crown forces. In turn, Horace Plunkett wrote the following to Elizabeth, Countess of Fingall:

The atrocities reported by the nuns in Foxford, and made the subject of a special enquiry by the military authorities at my request, prove to have occurred substantially as stated by the Reverend Mother. The officer responsible is being severely dealt with. I feel that my intervention in the case, and Sir Nevil having dealt with it personally, renders it improper to make any propagandist use of the facts.[22]

Elizabeth recalled the story, told to her by a Sister of Charity, of the great pride Agnes felt when she heard that someone in a London drawing room had spoken of 'this little nun's audacity in defying the British Army and asking "Who is this nun?"' Elizabeth herself was present and she stood up and answered:

You need not query anything Mother Bernard says. If it comes from her it is true, and her motives are unassailable.[23]

Agnes thought it very courageous of Elizabeth to defend a friend under such circumstances.

However, it was the Civil War that would prove to have the most disastrous effect on Foxford and its people:

For four months as the civil war raged, Foxford had become completely cut off when the bridge over the River Moy and the bridges at Cloongullane, near Swinford and Ballylahan, near Foxford had been blown up. On Saturday July 15th the *Irish Times* reported that Foxford is completely isolated by the Irregulars and food supplies are running short.[24]

The mill had no postal or rail service. Large stocks of material began to build up. In June 1922 Agnes announced the indefinite closure of the woollen mills. She had little choice but to act as she did. She instructed the local curate to read out a notice of the shutdown at all Masses in the town. The announcement also appeared in the local and national papers:

> Owing to the stoppage of trains and posts we are forced to shut down this mill until communications are opened again and normal business conditions resumed. We have already large stocks on hands and we cannot afford to increase same.[25]

The Irish Times reported:

> The Providence Woollen Mills have been closed pending the return of normal conditions. 300 men and women have been thrown out of employment.[26]

Agnes expressed her disappointment to the Mother General:

> After struggling so hard for the last thirty years and keeping it open in spite of the War and the Black and Tans, it is our own Irishmen who are bringing poverty into this locality. In another fortnight many poor men with large families depending on their weekly wages in the mill will be starving.[27]

A letter from Joseph J. Kelly, the representative of the woollen mills in Australia, appeared in the *Irish Independent* expressing exactly the same sentiments as Agnes and condemning the 'misguided Irishmen' who had allowed their country to sink into anarchy:

> It is with feelings of deep regret that I noticed the closing down of the Foxford Mills. As I am the Australian representative of that mill since 1914, it has been a puzzle to me why I was receiving no reply to two letters I posted to the Secretary

over four weeks ago. The article in your paper explains it all. During my eight years' business correspondence with Foxford, including the submarine menace during the world's war, or later during the reign of the Black and Tans, not a letter of mine to the mill has miscarried or not been delivered. I arrived here last June from Australia, buoyed up by the hope that I was to see my native land free … and to return to the land of my adoption (where I could) do my bit pushing Ireland's industries on the Australian market. What a false dream! And who has shattered it? Misguided Irishmen.[28]

Some form of relief for the inhabitants of the town appeared on the horizon, when a few months later the anti-Treaty IRA left the town. *The Weekly Irish Times* captured the mood of the locals:

> The joy of Foxford knows no bounds as the regime of the Irregulars had threatened to ruin the woollen industry there. The village is bedecked with bunting in honour of the advent of the national troops. The providence mills that were obliged to close and thereby render three hundred hands idle, will shortly be working again. The district has however suffered in other ways, as many bridges across the Moy have been destroyed so that access to Foxford is a matter of extreme difficulty.[29]

Michael Collins.

The woollen mill did reopen, but another tragedy caused it to close again on 28 August 1922. The closure was a mark of respect to General Michael Collins, who was ambushed and killed at Béal na Bláth in Cork on 22 August. Agnes did not close the mill in a blasé manner, but rather in deference to the man to whom she had sent a present of a Foxford rug some time before. She in fact had a special reason for sending the rug to Michael Collins. In 1921 she had planned to extend the mill and build a new chapel on the convent grounds, but she was prevented from doing so by both secular and religious authorities. Shortly after the signing of the Anglo-Irish Treaty in 1921, without any warning, she received clearance for work to begin on the building scheme. She figured only one man could have made this possible, and that was Michael Collins. He had made it clear that he intended to revitalise Ireland's undeveloped industrial base:

> If our national economy is put on a sound footing from the beginning it will, in the new Ireland, be possible for our people to provide themselves with the ordinary requirements of decent living. It will be possible for each to have sufficient food, a good home in which to live in fair comfort and contentment. We shall be able to give our children bodily and mental health; and our people will be able to secure themselves against the inevitable times of sickness and old age ...
>
> The industries we possess are nearly all capable of expansion. We can improve and extend all the following: Brewing, distilling. Manufacture of tobacco. Woollen and linen industry. Manufacture of hosiery and underclothing. Rope and twine industry. Manufacture of boots and shoes, saddlery, and all kind of leather articles. Production of hardware and agricultural machinery. Production and curing of fish.[30]

The rug was a one-off, woven in pure unprocessed wool in green, white and gold, the colours of the Free State. It was known as a 'knee rug' and was used in pony-traps and motor cars during this period:

> It was sent as part of a larger consignment of goods to Dublin by the Woollen Mills and was packaged separately with no identification label and addressed simply to Michael Collins, c/o Dublin Castle.[31]

When Michael Collins was ambushed, his body was taken to Shanakiel Hospital in Cork city. A blood-stained bullet-riddled carriage rug accompanied the body; this was the rug that Agnes had sent him. The *Western People* carried reported:

> The original rug seems to have disappeared. The nurse, who attended Collins after the ambush, gave the rug to a Cork solicitor in 1965. He later gave it to a priest who was researching the life of Collins. The priest, Fr. Twoegg, brought the rug to the attention of the Foxford Mills in 1990 [*sic*]. Later the priest gave the rug to the National Museum. It is understood that

Replica of the Michael Collins rug.

efforts to trace the rug have failed. Seventy-five years later, in 1997, to mark the 75th anniversary of Collins's death a replica of that rug would be produced again. It was labelled with a special Michael Collins Foxford Woollen Mills Label. The rug generated huge interest.[32]

Bridget Gallagher recalls that:

Michael Collins got a rug one week before he died. Michael Collins was here. He got a rug with the map of Ireland on it. He went up to Castlebar to visit his sister who was a teacher. He wore a jacket with leather elbows and it took off for a while. It became the fashion. Michael Collins was the first one to wear them. When he was killed he had the rug on his lap. This woman washed the rug; she found out that it was made in Foxford. So they rang Foxford for the pattern to see if Foxford had it. A couple of years ago in America they wanted a Michael Collins rug again for the film so they made a good lot of them.[33]

Ivars Zauers had an interesting story regarding the original Michael Collins rug. When it was returned to the mill, in the late 1980s, he did an analysis of it. He said:

The rug was made in an unusual way; it was made of three fine yarns instead of one thick yarn. It was woven in a green heather mix with white and gold thread. The rug had not been washed, and the holes could be bullet holes or moth eaten ones, there were dark stains on it, possibly blood.[34]

The rug was given to the National Museum in Dublin, but unfortunately it disappeared and there is no record of it at present.

After Collins' death the war dragged on and atrocities were committed by both sides. It was a futile affair, with many suffering cruel injuries and much loss of life.

> It was clear by the end of spring that the Free State forces were massing for a final solution … Frank Aiken new IRA Chief-of-Staff declared a unilateral ceasefire on 30th April. [W. T.] Cosgrave [President of the Executive Council of the Irish Free State] rejected any peace proposals which did not include decommissioning of arms held by the IRA and he could not by the accepted constitution permit republican TDs who had not taken the oath of allegiance to sit in the Dáil. Any continuation of the struggle was now accepted as murderous folly. On 24th May, Frank Aiken, Chief-of-Staff ordered anti-Treaty forces still in the fields to dump arms.[35]

Carmel McCaffrey summarises the situation:

> The Anti-Treaty side knew that it could not win, peace was at last restored and the Civil War ended in May 1923 when the IRA laid down arms and gave up the fight. Figures for the total number killed in the Civil War vary, but more lives were lost than in the War of Independence.[36]

When the war ended, it must have been welcome news to Agnes and her workers, who had felt its impact greatly.

Success

THE MILL WAS often subject to audits because of the grants given by the CDB. One man who visited in 1894 was a Mr W. J. D. Walker of Glenbanna Mills, Laurencetown, County Down, who had invented a modern handloom. He acted as a part-time salaried adviser to the Congested Districts Board (CDB) in relation to the woollen industry in Foxford. In his report to the CDB he stated:

> I understand it is only some two and a half years since the factory started, and I confess I was very much surprised at the progress which had been made in so short a time. In a manufacturing district the starting of a Mill is often a simple matter of so much building and engineering work, the putting down of machinery, and the employing of workers, the great proportion of whom are trained. The difficulties incident to management, economical production, and financial success are ordinary. In a place like Foxford the difficulties are extraordinary. Where everyone requires to be taught everything and all at the same time, the management would require to be omnipresent. The production per worker is at the lowest possible point, the quality of the goods they are capable of producing is the commonest and most un-remunerative – even these will be defective involving claims. Economical production is impossible the total turn off is contracted within the narrowest limits, expansion being impossible till workers are trained ... My opinion is that

the outlook for Foxford is most hopeful, and the business will soon be established upon a solid commercial basis. It would be impertinence in me to characterise the business capacity of the Lady Superioress, Mrs Morrogh-Bernard, the ladies under her, and the hard-working manager. Your Board is under the deepest obligation to them, and while your capital has contributed, they are the real benefactors of the neighbourhood. I shall conclude by saying that I have my northern prejudices, just as markedly accentuated as most men, and if the above report is favourable, it is not because I went there to praise what I saw, but because I have stated nothing but what I believe to be true.[1]

In similar fashion Mr George Thomson of Huddersfield visited the mill at the request of the CDB and made the following report:

I was very much interested and agreeably surprised with my visit to Foxford. I found already in good working order a manufactory established on what I consider to be fairly up-to-date principles of manufacture, engaged in the production of goods for which there is large demand.[2]

The CDB seemed quite pleased with the progress of the mill and reported:

The repayment instalments that have since fallen due have been punctually paid. During the past year these factories (Foxford and Ballaghaderreen) have been visited by most of the members of the Board, and they were much pleased with the progress made, and with the kind of goods that they saw in process of manufacture. At Foxford, however, a serious difficulty arose with respect to the water power by which the factory is worked, it being contended that the mode of taking the supply for the factory was injurious to fishery and landed riparian interests.

The mediation of this Board was accepted by those concerned, and a plan which was devised by M. Robert Manning, C.E., was satisfactory to all concerned. The works were most successfully carried out at a cost of about £780 under the direction of M. Max Green, C.E.; and the Board decided to defray this amount, having regard to the heavy expenditure already incurred by the promoters of this promising industrial undertaking.[3]

The fact that a solution to the problem had been found congenially and that she didn't have to bear the cost must have been music to Agnes's ears. That the CDB offered to do this shows the esteem in which it viewed the industry. However, another visit to the mill proved more contentious. In her memoirs Agnes recalls:

Early in August 1896, two Yorkshire milling experts came, by invitation of Mr. Balfour, to report on our work for the CDB – a Mr. Slater of Ashville, Farsley and Providence Mills, Stanningley, and Mr Samuel Law of Cleckheaton – Messers Kennedy & Micks arrived from Dublin to meet them and hear their opinion. These gentlemen assured them they had no suggestions to make. Our work was thoroughly satisfactory. This inquiry had resulted from an application we had made to the CDB for a further Capitation Grant, so badly required for all we aimed at doing. Soon afterwards a long article relative to this visit appeared in a Yorkshire paper – sympathetic in tone and quoting a good deal from our Booklet, but making statements concerning the backwardness of Mayo which might have been left unsaid. It gave readers to suppose that our people were at best but semi-civilized, that in summer-time they discarded most of their clothes; and in very hot weather, the men went almost nude. We were also told that on our arrival here there were no two-storey houses in the locality, and the people did not know how to go up and down stairs.[4]

What follows is an extract from the article:

Quite a new phase of life – and an exceedingly interesting one, too, was revealed to Mr. Charles H. Slater, of Ashville, Farsley and Providence Mills, Stanningley and Mr Samuel Law of Cleckheaton, during a visit they made recently to Foxford in County Mayo, in order to investigate on the behalf of the Irish Congested Districts Board and report to that useful body in response to an invitation from Mr. G. W. Balfour, M.P., the Chief Secretary of State for Ireland. Unless they noticed a reference to it in Parliamentary reports, some of our readers will probably never have heard of Foxford. Indeed half a dozen years ago few people seem to have been aware of its existence; and it is to be hoped that a still less number know the extent of destitution then prevailing in the locality, for if they did know, the neglect to endeavour to remedy it could be little less than criminal. Foxford is only 150 miles from Dublin, but a description of the conditions under which the Irish people lived there, before a band of noble-hearted nuns began to work amongst them, reminds one of travellers' tales of life far beyond the pale of civilization in foreign lands, and could not be credited respecting a district a few hours journey from England, grown up people would be unaware how to go up and down ordinary steps! Yet five years since these nuns found that the natives of Foxford had never seen any stairs; they had lived only in little cabins, and there were no two-storied buildings in the locality. With much hesitation, they ventured to go up steps, but they had [no] notion of walking down. Grown-up men and women descended like little children here, though hardly do [so] easily, sitting on each step; the nuns could always tell when anybody was coming downstairs by the continuous, 'bump, bump, bump!'

In the Foxford district the people were indeed semi-civilized. In summer, they preferred to cast off most of their clothing and in very hot weather men thought nothing of going about almost quite nude. But notwithstanding their backwardness in many respects, and despite the fact that they were almost always on the verge of starvation, the potato being their staple diet, these Irish peasants were very proud, in a sense. When the nuns started a woollen factory and technical schools in connection with a convent, the grown up people refused for a while to do any work in the mill. They thought factory-life was beneath them and they preferred to go on living in their own careless hand-to-mouth way. But gradually they realised that 'there was money in it,' and some of them responded to the invitation given so kindly and so frequently. Recognizing that the best work could be done with the children, the nuns from the first devoted special attention to them. There were only two classes amongst the people – viz, children and aged folks; the young men and women, those in the prime of life, had gone to America, whence they sent money that sometimes enables their relatives at home to avert keen distress.

The Englishmen were astonished with the factory. Naturally, they had expected finding that the machinery was rather out of date, whereas it proved to be equal to that in many of the mills in England. When a new speed-tester was produced as likely to be useful, the Lady Superior, Mrs Morrogh-Bernard smiled and said they had one similar … The mill-books were shown to the visitors, who found that the nuns kept the accounts, etc. very neatly indeed, and quite in accordance with the system adopted in big concerns in this country. About 100 employees have been trained for millwork. Mr Max Green, C.E., Hon. Sec. of the Irish Textile Industries Association, has been an exceedingly useful friend of the Foxford enterprise. In the year 1890 the convent, the Technical Schools, and the woollen factory of Foxford, now the busiest hive of industry on Ireland's congested Western seaboard, were not in existence. Far back in the '70s various missionary bodies had called attention to the great need of a convent at Foxford. The Redemptionist Fathers in 1880 and the Franciscans in 1890 pronounced it to be one of the most forlorn and destitute districts they had ever visited and when Mr. Arthur Balfour inspected it in the latter year it furnished him with striking evidence that the voice from the West was no fraudulent or hysterical cry of 'Wolf!' raised to serve political or any other purposes. He started relief works at once, which went a good way to avert the threatened famine. That the deplorable state of things is to be laid entirely to the fault of nature, or to that mysterious pagan factor known as 'bad luck' is a question that is better left un-discussed.

Visitors to Foxford will see a state of thing perhaps unique of its kind in the world. They will see a mill yard 'manned' by a woman, vowed to poverty and un-worldliness, who shows as much energy and business capacity as those stimulated by personal greed, and in the mill hands, a staff of alert young men and women, among whom an unseemly word or coarse jest is never heard, who have become instinctively refined through living in the rarefied air which surrounds all communities and families of no matter what creed, class or degree of culture, who aim at a high ideal life – the life transcending the claims of self. The difficulties and disasters, the checks and reverses, the objections alike of friend and foe, which had to be lived through in starting and then steering the big undertaking, are now matters of history in the neighbourhood where the Sisters of Charity are so reverenced and beloved. Providence sent them many kind patrons and warm sympathisers, Protestant as well as Catholic. The earnings of the boys are placed in the Post Office Savings Bank to start a nest egg for the future. 'One is inclined to wonder that in the quiet seclusion of our convents the movement for the revival of Irish Industries should find its most ardent supporters,' says a writer in the *New Ireland Review*. 'We have been accustomed to see in the religious sisters the teachers of our little ones, the comforter of the afflicted and of the dying. But we could hardly have expected to see them boldly enterprising in the apparently forlorn task of giving life to our dead industries.' That the nuns have been successful as well as enterprising Mr. Slater and Mr. Law were convinced.[5]

Agnes recorded the visit in her notes, writing that 'travellers' tales can be wonderful'.

In 1896 a Cottiers exhibition was held in Foxford. Agnes recalls:

> Lady Cadogan arrived from Dublin and was accompanied to Foxford by Lord and Lady Lucan and Lord and Lady Arran. She opened the Cottiers exhibition. There was music and entertainment and the newspapers correspondent Miss O'Connor Eccles wrote favourably of it in the *Sunday Times*. Much good came of the exhibition and the CDB sent another grant for eggs.[6]

Lady Cadogan.

'Cottier' was the term used for a person who was the occupier of a cabin with little or no land attached. With Agnes in charge, however, the cottiers were more than capable of exhibiting their products. *The Connaught Telegraph* carried an account of the exhibition:

> Last year the Sisters of Charity in Foxford startled everybody by the daring enterprise of a Connaught Exhibition and achieved a success truly marvellous. The cottiers show this year is a no less worthy move being confined to cottiers within a radius of five miles of Foxford ... The Foxford cottier has developed under the fostering care of the nuns into a new man with ideas and projects hitherto of which he knew nothing. The luxury of clean surroundings, the value of improved poultry, and the profit of a kitchen have been impressed on him, and he has proved an apt pupil. Close on 400 entries for gardens within a 5 mile radius of Foxford show what influences were at work and with what effect. The entries in the poultry section are also numerous. To those who have not seen Foxford within the past few years, the changes can hardly be realised. All that the good nuns would wish may not be yet accomplished but with the disadvantages under which they worked they can show wonderful results. To make the cottier work and then teach him to love the work he does has been the object of the nuns. The unique attempt of a Cottiers Show where cottier vies with cottier and where public interest can be centred in their efforts, and where the spirit of rivalry stirs up to increased effort was a useful and far-seeing conception. Such an attempt was reserved for Foxford and is the offspring of a fertile brain and a very kindly heart.[7]

Elizabeth, Countess of Fingall, in the book *Seventy Years Young*, which she collaborated on with Pamela Hinkson in 1937, recalled an incident the following year when Agnes proved herself to be a true champion:

> In August 1897 the Duke and Duchess of York paid a state visit and toured Ireland. I was asked to meet them at Adare, Co. Limerick, for the Royal visit. The party was a very small one, Gerald and Betty Balfour, Lord and Lady Castletown, Lord Roberts, Nigel Kingscote, Derek Keppel and Lady Eva Dugdale. I had brought two coats and skirts back from my German visit, one green and the other Parma violet colour, in light and very bright tweed. I wore them at Adare and they were much admired by the Duchess of York. Of course, Lady Fingall, these are Irish? I felt terribly ashamed and stuttered evasively, Oh, Ma'am I always try to wear Irish Industries. Then the Duchess and all the ladies of the party asked me to get them similar tweed. Nemesis! I wrote at once to every tweed manufacturer in Ireland to see if they could produce the stuff. Luckily there were hems to my skirts for me to cut patterns from. The material was an unusual light hopsack. None of the manufacturers could produce it. But, Mother Morrogh-Bernard at Foxford saved the situation. Wonderful woman! She had it specially made for me and delivered within a fortnight. She asked then if this new Foxford line might be called Fingall tweed. Of course I was much honoured.[8]

Switzer's department store in Dublin was the sole agent for Fingall tweed:

> The relationship between the Providence Woollen Mills and Switzer's department store in Dublin was clearly demarcated in Switzer's advertisement that appeared in *Lady's Pictorial* in which Elizabeth, Countess of Fingall allowed her photograph to unite fashionable tweed with Switzer's ... Agnes had responded

to a request by Elizabeth to copy the fabric in tweed garments she had purchased in Germany.[9]

Specialities in
Irish Manufacture.

FINGALL TWEEDS
(Registered).

Sole Agents, SWITZER & CO., Ltd.

These justly celebrated tweeds are now produced in reduced weights and cashmere finish to suit present dress requirements. They have more claim than ever to be called "the most beautiful of Irish fabrics."

REAL IRISH CROCHET LACE.

SWITZER & CO., Ltd., employ over one hundred and thirty workers in the manufacture of this most beautiful and fashionable lace. The gracious desire expressed by Her Majesty the Queen, that only British manufactured goods may be worn at the Coronation, has given an immense impetus to the demand for Irish Lace, and from the Continent and America SWITZER & CO., Ltd., have constant appeals through their agents for **MORE IRISH LACE**.

CROCHET COLLARS, 6/6 to 7 Guineas.
CROCHET LACE, from 3 in. to 22 in. wide.
HANDKERCHIEFS, with borders of Crochet Carrickmacross
Applique, Limerick, and Tambour.
LAPPETS, SCARVES, &c.

Goods sent for inspection to any part of the Kingdom on receipt of cash, or a satisfactory trade reference.

SWITZER & CO., Ltd., GRAFTON STREET, DUBLIN.

The Countess of Fingall in a Switzer's advertisement,
Lady's Pictorial *(8 March 1902).*
Courtesy of Toronto Reference Library

Agnes must have been very proud supplying the high echelons of society with the products of her fledging industry, but they were not the only ones who benefitted from her support. After the foundation of the Sisters of Charity in 1815, the Stanhope House of Refuge for young female orphans was established on 2 February 1819. Agnes had spent some time in Stanhope Street, so it must have been a proud moment for her when the centenary celebrations of the school took place:

> For the centenary celebrations in 1915 green uniforms of Foxford tweed from the Sisters' factory in Mayo were worn, with a garden party, fireworks and the Artane Boys' Band playing in spite of War, Rebellion and Troubles in Dublin.[10]

How fitting a tribute to Agnes that the pupils of her old school should wear a uniform she was responsible for creating.

Agnes was always grateful for help of any kind. She was a firm believer that assistance, as long as it benefited her people, was always welcome:

> Amongst recent visitors to the factory were Mr Doran, Inspector to the Congested Districts Board and Mr Michael Davitt, MP, both of whom expressed themselves highly pleased with it. Mr Davitt, the Sisters were glad to acknowledge, had been of considerable assistance to them. Pieces of goods of any colour, shape, or size are as welcome gifts at the factory as if the gifts came in the shape of money, for with these pieces, clothes are made for the poor workers and for the school children. Mrs Morrogh-Bernard believes she will succeed in her project; it certainly will not be her fault if she does not, but she relies on the co-operation of generous friends and a friendly Government. Her last words to your representative were, 'If we can succeed in this congested district of Foxford a similar project ought to be made a success in any other part of the country.'[11]

A report in the *Belfast News Letter* shows Agnes's response to a donation raised at a function held in Belfast for the relief of distress in the West:

> Mr Martin J. Burke, one of the treasurers of the recent subscription dance in the exhibition hall, the proceeds of which were devoted to the relief of distress in the West of Ireland, has received letters of acknowledgment and thanks for donations for £20 each from Rev. Dr. Lyster, Roman Catholic Bishop of Achonry, County Mayo; Most Rev. Dr. O'Donnell, Letterkenny, Roman Catholic Bishop of Raphoe, and Sister Agnes Morrogh-Bernard, Superioress, St Joseph's Place, Foxford, County Mayo. The last named writes: the more fortunate

dwellers in the North and East of Ireland have no idea of the chronic poverty and want prevailing in the South and West. The people have become so inured to it, that it is only in the last extremity the cry of distress is wrung from them, and patient endurance has become a kind of second nature to them.[12]

In later years the Foxford name made its way into the royal household as this extract from the *Western People* shows:

> The Princess of Wales and her daughters have recently invested in a number of the natural coloured hand woven shawls produced by the girls employed in the new Industry started at Foxford, Co. Mayo. The Princess also purchased one of the national long cloaks in Irish frieze conveniently provided with a capacious pocket hidden rather low down under the left front. On the slightly gathered shoulders falls the characteristic circular hood, lined with silk. These and other Irish manufactures were shown at the Irish Industries Depot, Motcomb Street, Belgravia, London.[13]

The Irish Industries Depot was a centre from which London businesses could purchase Irish-made goods:

> Lady Aberdeen, in setting up the Irish Industries Association, could bring the home, cottage and other industries of Ireland into some sort of working order, and to organise the sale and transition of goods, which, however excellent they were, suffered from not being sufficiently known or up to date in their design.[14]

One of the department stores where the ladies of London society purchased their goods was J. J. Fenwick's. There was a political slant to the support of Irish materials that Fenwick's identified in an advertisement in the *Gentlewoman* in January 1897:

Good news for Ireland, Irish Homespuns are to be the prevailing fashion for early spring coats and skirts. This delightful change in fashion will be of infinitely more practical benefit to Irish peasants than Home Rule.

FENWICK. New Creations
for Intermediate Season.

Delightful Change of Fashion for COATS and SKIRTS.

GOOD NEWS FOR IRELAND.

Advertisement for J. J. Fenwick of New Bond Street, London in The Gentlewoman, *30 January 1897.* © British Library Board

The advertisement connected the sartorial world to the highly contested political debates about Home Rule for Ireland while at the same time it promoted what could be called historical fair trade. The delightful fashions relied on tweed from three non-profit-making organisations: the Lucan or Castlebar tweed industry, Ardara tweed from Donegal, and Foxford tweed. All three producers avoided the use of middlemen in an attempt to return profits to Irish cottagers, aimed for a niche market and exhibited under the broad umbrella of the Irish Industries Association.[15]

The *Evening Telegraph* ran with the following item:

> Lady Aberdeen, in her elegant shop in Motcomb Street, Belgravia is bringing everything that clever Irish fingers make within reach of English buyers.[16]

In 1900 Muriel Gahan, later a champion of rural women and craft workers, moved to Castlebar with her family. Her father, Townsend Gahan, was an inspector with the CDB, and she wrote of travelling with him when she was a young child:

> To the desolate and isolated countryside north of the Nephin mountains, stretching from the Belmullet, Erris district coast line in the north west to the Foxford area in the east. Our method of transport was always the same, for short distances, our own pony and trap, and on longer journeys Mr. Ainsworth hired an 'outside car' with a tougher horse than our poor old Dolly. No feeling of cold because we were well wrapped up in our favourite Foxford rugs.[17]

The Gahans, while living in Castlebar, visited Foxford frequently and Townsend Gahan remained a friend and admirer of Agnes until she died.[18]

Another lady who had a treasured Foxford rug in her possession was Maire McEntee, daughter of Frank McEntee, who would later become Mrs Conor Cruise-O'Brien. In her autobiography, *The Same Age as the State*, she recalls feeling at home while a student in Paris:

> In my small student's room, where I felt peculiarly at home, with my books on their shelves, my Dufy print on the wall and my Foxford rug on the bed.[19]

The mill continued to go from strength to strength and by November 1910, when it had completed all the repayments to the CDB, it had earned both a national and international reputation for the quality of its products.[20] Agnes wrote:

> The last instalment of the CDB loan was paid off, and that same month Mr Thompson began work on the improvements to the Mill. He erected lofts to carry the carding engine and mules and an addition to the burling and finishing rooms.[21]

In the same year the CDB paid tribute to Agnes and her manager, Frank Sherry:

> For her business capacity and enthusiasm at first, and subsequently to the able assistance of Mr Frank Sherry, the manager of the factory, the unqualified success of this undertaking is due.[22]

Agnes was never one to rest on her laurels, and was constantly seeking ways in which to develop and improve her industry. Imelda Turnbull, granddaughter of Thomas Turnbull, said:

> At the beginning of the twentieth century, Agnes contacted the Galashiels Combined Technical School in Scotland which was started in 1889. It is thought she asked if a professional wool designer could be sent to Foxford to train a designer with a view of introducing some new patterns. Thomas Turnbull, my grandfather, was a lecturer at the Technical School in Galashiels, and he arrived in Foxford in the early 1900s. He did not intend staying, but for whatever reason, he did. He worked as the designer and introduced colour to the factory's products. He went on to train a young worker, Jack Dorr.[23]

There is an entry in the Census of Ireland 1911 listing Thomas Turnbull as a wool designer, and he and his family as residents of Foxford. Sadness came into the Turnbull family when Thomas's wife, Bridget, died in 1907. Imelda Turnbull recalled, 'Later he married a Bridget Brogan from Knockmore. My grandfather died in 1936 and is buried in Craggagh cemetery near Foxford.'[24]

Bernadette Kimmerling (née Dorr) confirmed:

> My father, Jack Dorr, went to Galashiels in Scotland and trained as a textile designer. He worked at the mill in textile management. He won medals at various exhibitions for his work.[25]

The woollen mill continued to grow:

> New designs in colourful tweeds and plaid patterned rugs were added to the white báinín wool fabrics and white blankets. The Mill's diverse production of flannel, frieze, kerseys, tweeds, clerical clothes, shawls and plaid blankets were noted at trade exhibitions throughout Ireland and England, winning plaudits for their quality and design.[26]

The mill came in for special praise from Charles Reid in his critique of the work carried out during the first five years of the CDB:

> It is a model in its workings, fitted up with the latest machinery and turning out the best quality of stuffs in tweeds, serges, blankets etc. There is certainly no fault to be found with the management or the excellence of the fabrics. Over forty women were paid at an average rate of six shillings a week, however, Reid was of the opinion that the commercial aspect could be

improved by employing commercial travellers to eke out suitable markets for the products. By 1900 two travellers were employed, one in England and one in Ireland, with the result that the demand exceeded the output of the factory. About 4,000 yards of tweeds, serge, flannels and blankets were produced weekly, and over one hundred were employed all year round on good wages. In addition about £3,000 was spent annually in the purchase of wool from local growers while £4,000 was paid for imported fine yarn.[27]

The success of the mill can be attributed to Agnes having the courage and initiative to act upon a venture in which she put total trust in providence. It must be said, however, that Agnes worked alongside providence, never missing an opportunity which would advance her cause. This was evidenced in a report carried by a London newspaper:

It has transpired that during her stay so far in Dublin, her Majesty has had sent to her for inspection specimens of many of Ireland's manufacturers. One of the most interesting displays she has yet seen was the work of Industrial classes aided, and in many cases formed, by the Congested Districts Board, which has done so much for the development and improvement of the terribly poor districts along the Western seaboard. There were also sent to her Majesty specimens of the products of manufacturers who have been encouraged and assisted by the Board in carrying on factories in the scheduled districts. The exhibits included homespun knittings from Donegal; beautiful costume cloths and suitings from Foxford, Co. Mayo; machine knittings from Ballaghedrin [*sic*]; hand knitting from Co. Mayo … Her Majesty showed great interest in the exhibits, and made a considerable number of purchases.[28]

An undertaking like this would have deterred a less courageous person. Fr Tom Finlay summed it up very succinctly:

> One day, a happy day for Foxford and its neighbourhood, a Sister of Charity stood upon the bridge of Foxford surveying the bleak and dreary landscape which it commands. She had a quick eye for evidences of human misery, and they abounded before her. Her life work lay in haunts of poverty. She had made intimate acquaintance with it in city slums and backward rural districts; but here was a field for her ministry more forlorn than any in which she had laboured. Her ambition was stirred. To carry hope into the cheerless cabins, to uplift the souls which their squalor degraded, to diminish the suffering which they housed – this was an enterprise worthy of the service to which she was vowed and would be to the mind of the Master she served. She could count on self-devotion like her own among the Sisterhood to which she belonged. With these resources she would undertake the enterprise, strong in the conviction that to the Power on which she relied all things are possible.[29]

The hope and trust Agnes placed in providence had been constant. Such a great belief shows the strong and unwavering faith that accompanied all things Agnes undertook in the name of a greater power.

Famous Visitors to the Mill

A VISIT BY Lady Aberdeen, wife of the Lord Lieutenant of Ireland, to Foxford captured the attention of the press and many others. Lady Aberdeen arrived on 14 July 1893 on her way back from the Chicago World's Fair, which had opened on 1 May 1895 and where she had established an Irish Village. She gives an account of her journey in the book *We Twa*:

> A final trip to Ireland for business purposes had to be fitted in, as there were a number of industries in the West and North to be visited in connection with the Irish Village. I started my tour with Mr and Mrs James Talbot Power of Leopardstown Park, who gathered all kinds of people to talk over plans for promoting prosperity and industrial welfare in Ireland. Among these, Horace Plunkett was always to the fore, and many were the talks about his scheme of a Department of Agriculture and Technical Instruction, which afterwards materialised.[1]

In her memoirs Agnes wrote:

> Visit to the Mill of Lady Aberdeen, President of the Irish Industries Association, the object of which was to encourage and help small industries and bring them into touch with the world markets.[2]

Addressing the crowd at the woollen mill, Lady Aberdeen said:

> We are very rejoiced to hear of the success which has attended
> the Rev. Mother's efforts. I know she would be the first to say
> how she has been helped by many kind friends and the interest
> they have taken in her work, but we all know her and thoroughly
> feel that if it had not been for Mother Morrogh-Bernard these
> mills would not exist today. I am glad indeed to have this
> opportunity of joining with her many friends in congratulating
> her on the success of her labours, and in presenting to her
> the very best wishes of all who are connected with the Irish
> Industries Association for her very great and noble work. And
> let me thank you sincerely, ladies and gentlemen; and you
> who have been good enough to give me this address from the
> workers themselves, may I congratulate you on having the good
> fortune of belonging to Foxford, because in the time to come
> you will be very proud to be amongst those who started these
> mills, and to have been the first to reap the advantages which
> your good Rev Mother has placed within your reach.[3]

*Workers in the mill, 1893. This photograph was taken during Lady Aberdeen's
visit.* Courtesy of Lord Aberdeen (taken from Lady Aberdeen's papers)

Lady Aberdeen had founded the Irish Industries Association in 1886 to help improve and develop all home industries, including dairy and poultry, rabbit- and bee-keeping.[4] She felt that promoting indigenous industries would encourage self-sufficiency and help to combat the dire poverty that was rife in the countryside, especially in the western regions.

> She was instrumental in establishing the Irish Village at the Chicago World's Fair opened on the 1 May 1893. The venture was put on a business-like footing by the appointment of Mr Peter White, manager of Michael Davitt's Woollen Company to undertake the whole business. He accompanied her on a final tour of industries during a fortnight of bleak February weather; he fell ill with pneumonia and died a few weeks before the Fair was due to open.[5]

When this happened, Ishbel (Lady Aberdeen) and her husband went themselves to oversee matters in Chicago. White's widow took his place and made an excellent job of it, but the presence of the Aberdeens added to the attraction of the Irish Village. Horace Plunkett was also heavily involved.

> President Cleveland paid a visit to the Irish section where he received the Earl and Countess of Aberdeen and a deputation of Irish lace-makers and dairy maids ... Lord Aberdeen gave the President a bunch of shamrock, a blackthorn stick and a lace handkerchief for Mrs Cleveland.[6]

Marjorie Pentland described the Irish Village:

> On the opening day, May 12th 1893 ... 20,000 visitors paid their twenty-five cents entrance fee to the Irish Village and

were captivated by the sight of the rosy colleens, and the sound of their musical brogue as they worked beside turf fires in the cottages, dispensed butter-milk and butter in the model dairy, danced jigs and recited Irish verse in the village hall. Throughout the six months of the Fair crowds grew and sales mounted. More medals of merit were awarded to the village than to any other exhibitor; it was one of only three such shows to make money. After the guarantors had been paid in full, it showed a profit of £50,000. The profits had flowed back into poor homes all over Ireland; a market for their industries had been established in America. Ishbel (Lady Aberdeen) had watched the pathetic pleasure of old Irish people as they went through the cottages and saw the familiar settles and dressers of their youth, or were persuaded to join again in a cross-roads jig or Irish reel. Since the Chicago idea crossed her mind two and a half years before, it had caused her many agitations. But the Irish Village had been useful to Ireland and when the Fair closed in October 1893, she wrote in her journal, so 'all's well that ends well.'[7]

Not only did the Irish Village make money, but Lady Aberdeen secured fresh outlets and orders for Irish goods because of it. Horace Plunkett, who worked with her in the Irish Industries Association, observed:

> One great secret of success [of the village] is the way [in] which Lady Aberdeen is advertised. Her name is all over the village – it is her village – the IIA. Jim Power [James Talbot Power, president of the committee] and the rest of us – I'm not jealous – have given our work and money to make Lady Aberdeen the best advertised lady in the work. Well, she works hard herself, and her work is mostly good.[8]

The Aberdeens travelled to Ireland at the end of May 1893 to report on the chances of the Irish Village and to seek out more craftwork for display there. A report in the *Huddersfield Chronicle* stated:

> Lord and Lady Aberdeen reached Queenstown on Saturday night, en route to England, on their return from Chicago, where Lady Aberdeen opened the Irish Village at the World's Fair. The Mayor of Cork and an influential deputation from Cork and Queenstown met the travellers and cordially welcomed them to Ireland. Lady Aberdeen stated that the Irish village proved a success and it was intended to apply the resulting funds to the development of cottage industries in Ireland.[9]

Lady Aberdeen inspired Davy Stephens, a newspaper seller at Kingstown and a much-loved character who greeted distinguished travellers as they landed on Irish soil, to mention her in his 'Davy's Kolum' in the *Kingstown Monthly*:

> Congratulated the Countess of Aberdeen on the great success of her benevolent tour through poverty-stricken districts of the West and North West.[10]

During her visit to Foxford Lady Aberdeen referred to the Irish Village exhibit:

> I am sure you would all like to hear that the Irish Village in Chicago is really and truly proving a very great success, financially and otherwise, and if the result is the financial success which we now count upon, we shall hope to have still further means of following Rev Mother Bernard's good example.[11]

Maureen Keane, in her book *Ishbel: Lady Aberdeen in Ireland*, observes that when Lady Aberdeen met the nuns in their polished parlours or surveyed the work in their institutions she was:

> meeting women with whom she had much in common. They all shared a belief in a Christian God, and they all worked to help those less fortunate than themselves. Also, though unlikely to have been acknowledged, there was the shared triumph of wielding a measure of power. Admittedly, Ishbel's power and status derived from that of her husband, while the power of the nuns was a different, and perhaps more hardly-won weapon, but power it was, and Ishbel was rapidly discovering its pleasures. She might only be the wife of the Lord Lieutenant but she was very much emerging as a person in her own right – and a popular one in Irish eyes foremost as she was in every good and kindly duty.[12]

Agnes had the admiration of many, some famous and some not so famous. One of her admirers was George Wyndham, Chief Secretary to Ireland from 1900 to 1903. He greatly admired the religious orders that worked among the poor in Ireland. He loved many of the western priests as they loved him. A visit to Foxford moved him very deeply. Charlotte Dease remembers being one of the party that went with him on that occasion:

> At Foxford, as usual, Agnes hid herself, and a charming and very pretty nun, who was the secretary, received the party. An introduction was made by way of 'The Chief Secretary of Ireland – the Secretary of Foxford.' The charming nun took the Chief Secretary over the mills and showed him everything.[13]

An account of this visit and how it affected Wyndham is given in Charles Gatty's book *Recognita*. Gatty said Wyndham poured out his soul to him about it, saying:

> And what do you think they have up over the altar in the Chapel? *Mitis sum et humilis corde* (I am meek and humble of heart). After all the clang and din of well advertised philanthropy, educational, agricultural and industrial restoration brought about by the Sisters of Charity and over all the divine inspiration – *mitis sum et humilis corde.*[14]

Aiden Quigley, in his book *Green Is My Sky*, tells of his grandfather's account of people who visited the mill:

Lord Cadogan.

> There were other visitors to the mill – Lord and Lady Cadogan came, also Sir Francis Cruise, and a young girl whose beauty I have not seen equalled or even approached. She arrived one day on an outside car, not as might have been supposed from her elegant appearance, to see if we had anything alluring for her to purchase, but as a sympathiser with the poor and the downtrodden. It was the year 1898 – once again the crops had failed and many parts of the country were in distress and the poor West most of all. The young girl who came personally to inquire into the trouble to the poor was Maud Gonne. She was the loveliest person I ever saw.[15]

Maud Gonne did indeed visit the mill and she wrote about her visit in an article entitled 'Foxford, What May Be Done', published in *The Freeman's Journal*:

The one cheering and encouraging spot I have seen in the congested districts is Foxford. It shows what may be done for the people if only a little interest is in view. It brings out all the more glaringly the criminal neglect of the English Government, on whom rests the entire responsibility for the misery and suffering of the peasants of the Western seaboard. What one noble woman has succeeded in doing, a feeling of indignation and shame comes over one that everywhere in the congested districts the same effort is not being made to improve the lives of the people, whose actual condition is a disgrace in any country which pretends to civilisation. The poor, patient enduring Mayo peasants, with wonderful sea-coloured hopeless eyes looking out from thin beautiful faces, what a grand race you might be, if only the hopelessness were not. If only you were given the want of developing your faculties and thinking of something beyond the grinding necessity of making every acre of stony, valueless land yield ten shilling to some worthless landlord who cares for you less than he cares for his cattle and his dogs.

It is seven years since the Reverend Mother, Mrs Bernard, and thirteen Sisters of Charity settled in Foxford, then dismal and wretched a place as any in the congested districts. It was just this wretchedness that decided the choice of these generous women. The beautiful Moy rushes through the Foxford valley, and the Reverend Mother saw at once how its water power might be utilised. She borrowed £14,000, and had erected a practical woollen manufacturer, a 'one set' woollen mill, with technical schools attached to it. But things did not run smoothly. Some local landlord declared that the works undertaken on the Moy infringed on his rights and would injure his fish, and foremost the wheels of the Foxford factory had to stand idle. But the nuns won the case, and today Foxford is a transformed place. I was interested in seeing the bright faces of the people and the bountiful tweeds, friezes, flannels, shawls, and blankets which they were turning out that one forgets to enquire if the fish had been very much inconvenienced. Some 130 people are employed in the factory and the technical schools, but this is only a small part of the work of these Sisters of Charity. They among the people have taught them how to make their homes cleaner and brighter; they offer clothes made in the factory for the best kept house, they give flower and vegetable seeds for the gardens. Even sanitary arrangements are not beneath their attention and I am told that 160 manure pits have been cleared away from the houses 'to please the nuns'. 'I sure do a great lot of work for the nuns,' said one man to me, pointing out a neat garden before his cottage, 'and now I am draining land for them.' They have introduced a knitting industry and poultry industry to help the people find markets for their produce. The convent sews all sorts, from coarse garments down to 'the daintiest ladies underwear'. All I saw there was beautifully finished. The Reverend Mother told me she was most anxious to get orders from shops for making large quantities of shirts, and underwear, so as to be able to give employment to more people. As I knelt for a moment in the pretty little oratory which had been once an outhouse, but which, like everything else at Foxford has undergone a magic transformation, Sister Mary whispered to me, 'You are kneeling where Reverend Mother kneels, remains a hero late into the night. Ah, she is a wonderful woman; you saw now the factory wheel which turns unceasingly and noiselessly in the dark water and which moves all the machinery, well Mother is like that wheel, she works silently, hardly ever appearing, but it is she moves all here, thinks and plans everything, she is the pivot on which all turns.'[16]

Another famous neighbour of the mill who visited Agnes was Michael Davitt. Fifty-three years previously and five miles away, he and his family had been evicted from their home in Straide because they could not pay the rent. Davitt had advised Agnes during the initial stages of its establishment and he was now able to visit and see the mill in operation. In a letter to his friend and party colleague William O'Brien, who lived near Westport, Davitt mentions a visit to Foxford:

> I cannot get away before the mail [car] on Friday morning. This will land me in Castlebar I presume time enough for the convention … I have promised to visit the little Woollen Mill started by the Sisters of Charity in Foxford. Saturday will be my only available time for this. I must get back on Saturday as there is to be a meeting of the Parliamentary Committee in the Shelbourne on Sunday evening.[17]

What a joyous occasion it must have been for Davitt to witness this industry flourishing in such an impoverished area.

Down through the years many famous people from Irish economic, cultural, social, political and religious life, as well as people from other countries, visited the mill. Cardinal Dennis Joseph Dougherty, of Philadelphia, whose parents came from the parish of Aughoose, in Erris, County Mayo, visited in 1935. The *Western People* reported:

> Cardinal Dougherty, accompanied by his Secretary Mgr Lambe, visited the Sisters of Charity last week and later was conducted around the famous Woollen Mills where he was much impressed by all he had seen.[18]

In 1938 the Bishop of Los Angeles visited:

> A distinguished visitor to Foxford on Friday last was most Rev. Dr. Cantwell, Bishop of Los Angeles. He was accompanied by

most Rev. Dr. Morrisroe, Bishop of Achonry, and Very Rev. Canon Roughneen, Adm. Ballaghaderreen, and was the guest of the Sisters of Charity of St John's convent. Subsequently, Dr. Cantwell made a tour of inspection of the Providence Woollen Mills, and was introduced to the manager, Mr. Sherry.[19]

Former President of Ireland, Mary Robinson, has a special affinity with the mill. Agnes's cousin Jane Morrogh, from Rathcooney, County Cork, married Captain William Orme Paget Bourke Esq., Mary Robinson's paternal great-grandfather, in 1865.

William Orme Paget Bourke, was a captain in the 18th Regiment of Foot. He served with the regiment in various garrison postings in Ireland. The 18th of Foot or Royal Irish Regiment was one of the oldest independent garrison regiments raised in Ireland. It was founded by the Earl of Granard in 1684.[20]

Jane Morrogh.

Captain William Orme Paget Bourke.

By the time his son Henry Charles (Mary Robinson's grand-father) was born in 1875:

> William had left the army. At that time the family lived outside the Co. Mayo village of Bonniconlon in a house called Oatlands, a solid three-bay Georgian house overlooking the broad sweep of the Ox Mountains.[21]

So here was Agnes's little industry she had started, elevated in size and status. Little did she think when she gazed at the churning waters of the Moy on her arrival in Foxford, on that dreary and desolate evening, that in years to come her industry would beckon so many from all walks of life. Her trust in Providence had proved well placed.

Challenge and Achievement

IT WASN'T ALL plain sailing for Agnes as she carried on with everyday life. A vitriolic attack on both her and the mill was launched by Rev. Oliver J. Hannay, rector of Holy Trinity Church, Westport, County Mayo, who wrote under the pseudonym of George Birmingham.

> Hannay was a Protestant, born in Belfast in 1865. After serving as curate in Delgany, Co. Wicklow, he came to Westport and served as the rector there from 1892 to 1913. Afterwards he transferred to the Church of England when he became the rector of Mells, in Somerset in 1924. He was Canon of Holy Trinity Church in South Kensington, London, when he died at the age of 84 in 1950.[1]

The attack on Agnes and her work features in his novel *Hyacinth*, published in 1906, where he launches a blistering attack on the wages being paid to employees at the mill, the financial help given by the CDB and the conditions in which the nuns lived at the convent. The story is about a young man named Hyacinth, who enrols at Trinity College in Dublin to study divinity, and who, after meeting with extreme nationalists, drops out of college and becomes a commercial traveller for a Mr Quinn, owner of a Protestant woollen mill in County Mayo. It is here he encounters the convent and the nuns at Robeen, which the author uses to represent the mill and the convent in Foxford. While on a train journey, Hyacinth encounters two young girls leaving for America:

'But aren't you sorry to leave Ireland?' 'Sorry is it? No but I'm glad!' 'Onny's always saying that there was nothing to be earned in the factory. And she got more than the rest of us. Wasn't she the first girl that Sister Mary Aloysius picked out of the school when the young lady from England came over to teach us? She was the best worker they had.' 'It's true what she says,' said Onny. 'I was the best worker they had. I worked for them for three years, and all I was getting at the end of it was six shillings a week. Why would I be working for that when I might be getting wages like Bridgy's [her sister] in America? What sense would there be in it? … There's few that earned as much as I did. Many a girl works there and has no more than one and ninepence to take home at the end of the week.'

Hyacinth began to understand how it was that Mr. Quinn was being hopelessly beaten. This was no struggle between an independent manufacturer and a firm fed with Government bounties. Mr. Quinn's rival could count on an unlimited supply of labour at starvation wages, while he had to hire men and women at the market value of their services. He had been sorry for the two girls when they got into the train. Now he felt almost glad that they were leaving Ireland. It appeared that they had certainly chosen the wiser part.[2]

Hannay discusses the luxurious furnishings in the convent and an exhibition held at the mill and he writes about the financial help given by the CDB:

Within the great entrance-hall were palms and flowering shrubs in pots or tubs. The mosaic flooring, imported from Italy, and a source of pride to all the Sisters, shone with much washing and polishing. The Madonna with the blue eyes and the golden crown, before which even Bishops crossed themselves, was less in evidence than usual, for the expected guests were mostly heretics. She stood retired behind the flower-pots and veiled her benignity with the leaves of the palms. Right and left of the hall stretched corridors, whose shining parquet invited the curious to explore the working-rooms and eating-rooms which lay beyond. The door of the chapel stood open, and offered a vision of simpering angels crowding the canvas of the altar-piece, a justly admired specimen of German religious art. Before it, dimly seen, two nuns knelt, types of conventual piety, absorbed in spiritual contemplation amid the tumult of the world's invasion of their sanctuary. Another door led to the garden. Here a fountain played into a great stone basin, and neat gravel walks intersected each other at sharp angles among flower-beds … [B]eyond the garden, blocked off from it by a white wall, lay the factory itself, the magnet which was drawing the great of the earth to the nunnery. Here were the workers, all of them bright young women, smiling pleasantly and well washed for the occasion. They were dressed in neat violet petticoats and white blouses, with shawls thrown back from their head; a glorified presentment of the Mayo woman's working dress. Here and there, a touch of realism creditable to the Reverend Mother's talent for state management, one sat in bare feet – not, of course, dust or mud stained as bare feet are apt to be in Connaught, but clean. The careful observer of detail might have been led to suppose that the Sisters improved upon the practice of the Holy Father himself, and daily washed the feet of the poor.[3]

The story unfolds:

The refreshments provided, if not substantial, were admirable in quality. There happened just then to be a young lady engaged, at the expense of the County Council, in teaching cookery in a neighbouring convent. She was sent over to Robeen for the occasion, and made a number of delightful cakes of extremely small expense. The workers in the factory had given the butter she required as a thank-offering and the necessary eggs came from another convent where the nuns, with financial assistance from the Congested Districts Board, kept a poultry-farm. The Reverend Mother dispensed her hospitality with the same air of generosity with which Mr. Clifford had spoken of providing capital for the future ecclesiastical factories.[4]

Agnes remained silent in the wake of the publication of *Hyacinth*. However, a letter by Fr Tom Finlay, her close friend, appeared in *The New Ireland Review* (formerly the *Lyceum*) entitled 'The Blight of Criticism', where he takes Hannay to task on the satirical content of the novel. The letter was published in the *Mayo News*:

> Mr Birmingham's book purports to be a novel, but it is obviously wanting in the characteristics of a work of fiction. In reality, it is an account of certain contemporary movements and certain contemporary figures in Irish public life accompanied throughout with biting strictures on the movements and the men. It may, we think, be safely said that of the personages and the institutions here enumerated Mr. Birmingham has not in his entire book a genuine good word to say. He finds in them only objects at which to level his cynical and contemptuous satire and distorts and caricatures them in order to make his ridicule more effective.[5]

Finlay continues, outlining the precise details of the nuns' arrival in Foxford and the subsequent founding of the woollen mill. He refutes Birmingham's allegation of 'starvation wages', quoting facts and figures that could only have come directly from Agnes herself:

> In the beginning wages were of course very low; in fact payments to the first workers were a charitable grant rather than an equivalent for value in work. But here, too, things are now on a normal footing. A girl who has learned her business at the loom can now earn £1 per week or over. There are 120 hands employed in the factory. The wages bill for last year was £4,989 showing an average wage of over 15s per week.[6]

A few weeks later *The Catholic Times* newspaper lambasted Hannay for this scandalous attack on the Foxford nuns and his 'lampooning' of the Catholic Church:

> The case in which Mr. Birmingham oversteps all bounds in his pleturb [*sic*] of the convent factory of Robeen. The details given to this institution can only apply to Providence Mills of the Sisters of Charity at Foxford, Co. Mayo; yet the circumstantial details referred to are accompanied by other details, which are absurdly untrue. We are compelled to condemn his portraiture of the convent factory as a scandalous calumny on the noble and unselfish women who have devoted themselves to the bettering of the poor people of Foxford.[7]

Mrs W. O'Brien described Hannay's book:

> Amongst the most wanton a novel pretending to describe what was going on at Foxford, and accusing the nuns of sweating their workers and taking advantage of their poverty. *Hyacinth*

was a bad action. The best excuse for the attack on Mother Arsenius is, as Father Gildea remarks, that the book is omitted in some official lists of Canon Hannay's books.[8]

Hannay did address at some length the criticism that had been levelled at him. In a preface to this third novel, *Benedict Kavanagh*, which was published in 1907, he wrote:

> My description of the convent factory of 'Robeen' has been applied by some of my critics to Providence Mills at Foxford. My 'Robeen' is not Foxford; nor, as these same critics somewhat illogically point out, is my convent the least like the Foxford convent. Still I now see that in certain particulars the circumstances of my 'Robeen' were too like those of the Foxford factory. I think it right, therefore, to state now that I believe the Foxford factory to have been started from a philanthropic and not a commercial motive, and that the wages paid in this factory are probably not below the standard usual in Connaught. Whether, even under the peculiar circumstances of the place, it was right to spend large sums of public money in subsidizing a business which, if successful, must come into competition, and does as a matter of fact compete in the open market with other unsubsidized commercial undertakings, is a question which my critics perhaps wisely, did not discuss, and which I therefore feel no need of touching here.[9]

Before replying to his critics, Hannay had contacted Horace Plunkett, who was vice-president of DATI, a member of the CDB and a close friend of Fr Finlay's in the IAOS, for information on the mill in Foxford. In a letter to Hannay dated 14 June 1906 Plunkett stated, 'I had an inquiry made by people I can trust.'[10] He gave almost identical information on the question of grants and loans but produced a different set of figures for the wages being paid: an average of 9s 6d, with some higher-paid workers earning between 10/- and £1 a week. He concluded by saying:

> You can safely say they pay the wages usual in Connaught, subject only to the qualification that usually no wages are paid in Connaught.[11]

Hannay then contacted the Rev. Theophilus Patrick Landy, rector of Foxford and Straide between 1896 and 1915, to see if he could make further enquires about the wages paid to the workers in the mill.

> The Rector replied on 17 October, 1906 saying that He found it impossible to get information that could be verified, stating that word has evidently been passed to say nothing.[12]

However, Masahiko Yahata, a Professor of Irish Literature at Beppu University, Japan, argues that:

> Those who scathed the novel *Hyacinth* misunderstood Hannay's true message … They overlooked the fact that Hannay blamed the Protestant Unionist authority as much as the Catholic Nationalist authority for their arrogance, hypocrisy and bigotry.[13]

Despite Hannay's vicious attack, which must have impacted greatly on Agnes, she was in no way hindered in the continuation of her work for the poor and impoverished of the district.

On 23 January 1907 another catastrophe occurred, which was to prove a major challenge for Agnes. That morning the people of Foxford were awakened by the mill bell ringing at

3.30 a.m. instead of the usual time of 6 a.m. This was no regular call to work but a call for help, as flames could be seen surging high into the air and getting higher by the minute. Kevin Sherry recalls his father, Jim, telling him that:

> Minutes after ringing the bell he went to open the mill gates and found a large crowd of people already gathered outside. Within half an hour some 200 locals were organised in an effort to keep the blaze confined to the area where it had originally broken out, the national school and the old corn store then in use as a yarn storeroom.[14]

A report in the *Mayo News* described vividly the scene faced by locals on that morning:

> The spectacle presented by the fire was terrifying. The blaze reached high into the Heavens, and glared along the waters of the Moy. The roofs cracked with terrific force, and for a time it seemed as if the Mill was doomed to entire destruction. The Upper Convent school, the Industrial school, and the yarn store were evidently at the mercy of the fire, and the people immediately set themselves to arrest the flames' progress and prevent them from reaching the mill proper. Willing hands were soon at work. A portion of the roofing was cut away and a good clear space existed between the fire and the mill. At great personal risk the men of the town ascended the roof, and removed the slates and timber and another party worked unremittingly in plying the blaze with water from the Moy. Many of the volunteers suffered from burns and wounds, caused by falling slates, bricks, etc. Fortunately no one received serious injuries, although the danger at times was indeed great.[15]

The damage was extensive. The *Mayo News* reported:

Our representative visited the scene of the outbreak on Thursday and found the old mill (yarn store), which was formerly the whole factory, a complete ruin. Nothing was standing but the walls. Abutting on the store building were the numerous other buildings in wood and iron, in which all the machinery stands. These buildings cover fully an acre, and most of them are roofed with tarred felt. The mystery is how these buildings were saved … [T]he fire at some points actually scarred the wood-work. The energy of the many willing workers beat back the destructive flames and saved the factory proper.[16]

Perhaps the saving of the buildings was due to Agnes's prayers. Gildea tells us that Agnes 'spent the entire morning in her chapel praying that Providence would save His matchbox'.[17]

God must have heard her prayers, because by 7 a.m. the fire had been brought under control and was extinguished in another few hours. A costing of the damage was undertaken, and James Laffey writes:

A final assessment of the damage put the overall cost at £8,000, including the loss of £3,500 in yarn supplies. The factory was insured at the time for £27,000 and the school had insurance to the tune of £2,000. But, even in 1907, insurance policies must have contained 'small print' as records from the time indicate that the cost of the damage was only partially covered by the insurers. While most of the material lost in the fire was immediately replaceable, some items could not be re-acquired with such ease. In the national school, the records of the past fifteen years had been completely destroyed while three pianos were also lost. The loss of the pianos must have come as a particularly cruel blow to Sr Dora Tyrell, who had laboured long and hard to procure those valuable instruments for her budding musicians. She would have to begin all over again, raising the necessary monies to purchase new pianos ... [B]ut even if the flames had destroyed the Infant's School; Sr Dora Tyrell's vision for Foxford remained intact. Her junior orchestra was emblematic of the entire town, young, vibrant and on the rise.[18]

After the fire, Agnes built a new school on the riverside and replaced the burnt-out ruins of the old corn store with a new yarn store for the mill. She had a sprinkler system installed and also switched from gas to electric light. Until her death she continued to have the mill building and machinery updated and improved:

> The only improvements she refused to make were those that might threaten the livelihood of her workers. She refused to install a tossling machine in the factory as this would deprive the older women who did that job of their source of income.[19]

It wasn't just industrial work that Agnes and her Sisters focused on. Under their guidance the cultural life of the town improved. An accomplished pianist in her youth, Agnes realised that one of the best ways to promote harmony and friendship among her workers was to encourage them musically:

> In 1897 two workers in the Mill, John Johnson, a turner, and Dick Harte, who worked in the finishing department, started a band. They acquired a few pipes and unearthed an old drum. Other boys were encouraged to join the group and so the Foxford Brass and Reed Band was started. Agnes made the first donation of £1. The band performed for Charles Kennedy, a member of the CDB, who subsequently sent them a cheque

for £25. John Johnson bought eight second-hand instruments at a cost of £15.10s. Mr Higgins, a band master from Dublin, was engaged to give lessons. In October 1897, Mr Robinson, who was also a band master, came to Foxford with his wife and family. To minimize expenses, Agnes arranged that Mr Robinson should give half of his time to the band and work in the factory for the other half. The band won the Connaught Brass and Reed Band Championships in 1898 after being in existence for only a year. The prize was a beautifully decorated mace pole, which was cherished by the band.[20]

Thanks to Agnes and her Sisters, music featured prominently in Foxford. The music school was built by Agnes in 1923 and was home to the town's young musicians and to the famous Foxford Brass and Reed Band, which had been established in 1897. She organised New Year concerts, where the Sisters and workers could give musical performances. The *Western People* reported on the talents of the mill workers:

> It was a real pleasure to witness the air of comfort and health which characterised all the workers, and to see how neatly and becomingly each girl was dressed in the handsome and substantial fabrics manufactured by themselves. The programme was excellently arranged and the various items given with an excellence which might do credit to more pretentious performers.[21]

How heartening it was then, when in 1996 the Foxford Brass and Reed Band celebrated its hundredth anniversary. The following piece appeared in the *Mayo News*:

> On Sunday October 27, the Foxford Brass and Reed Band will

celebrate the 100th Anniversary of its formation with a public recital in the mill centre. Mother Morrogh-Bernard made the first donation of £1 to the fledging band ... [S]ince then the band has been present for every important occasion in Foxford. In 1992 the band travelled to America where they participated in the New York St Patrick's Day parade and won an award for the best marching band.[22]

Agnes also established a dramatic society and held many concerts. She encouraged sporting activities and was instrumental in the building of a handball alley on the west bank of the river for the mill staff, and this has played an important role in the sporting life of the town. She encouraged participation of the mill workers in many sporting events and was very proud of their achievements. Her pride is evinced in this story told by Eithne Brogan:

> My mother worked in the mill and she remembers her First Communion. There were sports held to mark the occasion. [She remembers] Mother Morrogh-Bernard giving her a threepenny bit for winning a race in the sports. She raced down as far as Shraith Garbh.[23]

Eithne and her family had a long association with the mill. Eithne worked there and so did both her parents:

> My father, Tom Durcan, worked in the mill for over forty years. Over the course of his career he became chief dyer in the mill. My mother worked in the mill with Sr Peter Alcantara, who founded the Pioneer Society. I worked in the office with Sr Peter. I worked there from 1963 to 1969. It is remarkable that both my mother and I worked with the same nun.[24]

An active pioneer centre was established in Foxford by Sister Peter Alcantara, to which Cardinal Cullen referred. Diarmaid Ferriter observed that:

> Cardinal Cullen singled out the active Pioneer centre at the convent in Foxford. His niece, Sr Stanislaus Cullen, was a Sister in the community and he was in frequent contact with her. He lauded the work in Foxford as contributing to civic and patriotic pride, and helping to curtail emigration.[25]

Ferriter makes the point that:

> The Annals of the Sisters of Charity reveal for example, not just the work done by individual convents in instilling temperance through sodalities and retreats and pioneer recruitment but also that many wives and mothers appealed to the Sisters to use their influence with husbands or sons.[26]

Music and the Pioneer Association were both very close to Agnes's heart. These two causes were carried on long after Agnes's death. In an interview with Michael Stanton, who worked at the mill from the mid-1950s to the early 1960s, he remembered it as a place where music was very much to the fore. Michael worked first in the pattern department and later as an independent sales agent. He covered parts of Leinster, Connaught and Ulster (excluding the six counties). Stanton recalled that:

> Quite a number of drapery shops stocked tweed material which would be sold by the yard, and also the famous Foxford blankets and rugs. There was a great demand for these products at the time.[27]

Agnes need not have worried that her industry, or indeed any of the other things she had established, would flounder. Everything was carried on as she would have wished. Michael Stanton recalled that:

> Sr Peter Alcantara was very much involved in the warehouse and also in the music side of things. On applying for a job at the mill, being a musician and Pioneer greatly enhanced ones chances of obtaining it. Sr Peter, who carried on the music school, would give each band member a little present at the end of the recital. In my time at the Mill, the band master was a Derryman called Johnny Ward. He also worked in the office at the mill. Sr Peter organised weekend retreats for the workers and these were held in the oratory beside the convent.[28]

There is no doubt that Agnes and the Sisters influenced many young people in the Foxford area. In the book *Labourers in the Vineyard: The Religious of Foxford and Its Hinterland*, James Laffey states that:

> More than 100 young men and women from Foxford and its hinterland have pursued a religious vocation since the mid-1800s and each made an invaluable contribution to their church and their communities.[29]

A large number of those men and women had been educated at the national school in Foxford and then progressed to the secondary school staffed by the Sisters of Charity. Many of these young men and women went on to become exemplary figures in their respective communities throughout the world. One young woman who joined the Sisters of Charity was Teresa Doherty, who was born in Belgarrif, Foxford, on 15 December 1930. Sister Teresa:

is one of the last remaining heirs to the extraordinary legacy of Mother Morrogh-Bernard, who was inspired to open a Sisters of Charity convent in Foxford in 1891. Sixty years ago, the young Teresa Doherty was working in the Providence Woollen Mills – the industry founded by Mother Morrogh-Bernard – when she was inspired to join the Sisters of Charity. After she was professed in 1954 as Sr Margaret Ursula, she served in the Sisters of Charity convents in Kilkenny and Clonmel before being assigned to the Californian Mission as a teacher. She completed a master's degree in correctional counselling in the early 1970s. It was a career that was to open up a fascinating and fulfilling chapter in her life. She is the first to agree that had it not been for the influence of the Foxford Sisters of Charity all those years ago, she would not be where she is today counselling the troubled youth of California's ghettos.[30]

Andy Ruddy could certainly lay claim to having first-hand knowledge of the spirituality and work ethic of Agnes and her Sisters. The Ruddy family cottage was located on the site that later became the main entrance to the Providence Woollen Mills. His father, Tommie, was one of the first employees of the Sisters of Charity after their arrival in the town and he became a loyal supporter of Agnes. James Laffey writes:

> Tommie Ruddy was hired to supervise the social programmes initiated by Mother Morrogh-Bernard, who had been horrified at the poverty and unhygienic farming practices in Foxford and the surrounding districts ... [T]he programme for improvement would have been impossible to initiate without the support of Tommie Ruddy. He was akin to a modern-day agricultural consultant and Mother Morrogh-Bernard spared no expense in training the young man for his role, sending him to the Albert Agricultural College in Dublin, where he was educated in the latest farming methods.[31]

In 1946 Andy was ordained as Fr Bernard into the Society of the Divine Saviour and served in many areas of England and Wales. Fr Bernard was hounded by ill health and he died on 4 June 1978. He is buried in Wealdstone Cemetery near London. No doubt his relationship with the Sisters in Foxford was a guiding light throughout his life.

Mary and Kathleen Thornton were from a large family in Foxford town who had a long association with the woollen mill. They were sent to the local convent national school, where:

> They came under the influence of the Sisters of Charity. Among those whom they encountered in those years was the inspirational Mother Morrogh-Bernard, the foundress of the Foxford convent and mills.[32]

Both joined religious orders – Mary, the Religious of the Sacred Heart of Mary in Tarrytown, New York, and Kathleen, the Sisters of Our Lady of the Apostles, in Ballintemple, County Cork, in 1945. Mary was professed as Sister Bernard, and she became a highly recognised teacher of maths and science. Kathleen was professed as Sister Mildred and she undertook to serve in the missions in Ghana. However, her life was to be cruelly cut short when she and another Sister, Sister Jane, contracted typhoid fever:

> They had not even reached Africa when they were struck down with typhoid fever. On arrival in Ghana on August 24, 1946, they were immediately hospitalised in Cape Coast, where they hovered between life and death for several weeks. Sadly, Sr Mildred passed away on September 17 at the young age of 27 … One can only imagine the terrible sadness that was visited upon the Thornton family in Foxford on learning of Sr Mildred's

untimely passing. It was an era of limited communications, and families often learned of the death of loved ones without any prior warning of illness. The remains of missionaries were not repatriated in those days and Sr Mildred was laid to rest in Cape Coast, one of the many missionaries who had made the ultimate sacrifice in the quest to help the most disadvantaged people of the world.[33]

There were many religious, near and far, who had their character moulded in the humble surroundings of the Sisters of Charity. Those men and women inherited spirituality, a work ethic and a determination to help others akin to that of Agnes and her Sisters. They helped in so many different ways in faraway places scattered throughout God's earth.

Later Years

AGNES CONTINUED TO work for the betterment of Foxford until a few years before her death. One of her final projects as Superior in Foxford was the building of a proper convent chapel. Although she always wanted a worthy chapel for the convent, she was even more anxious that the needs of the poor be taken care of before such a large building project commenced. It was only when she was financially secure that she undertook the building of the chapel. It was designed by architect Professor R. M. Butler.

Agnes in later years.

Walking stick/seat used by Agnes.

The chapel design is based on the late Gothic style of the old Irish abbeys. Some of the stained glass windows were made by Earley's of Dublin and others were the work of Alfred Ernest Child.[1]

The foundation stone was laid in March 1923. Its rose window has the Eye of Providence as its centrepiece, which was the trademark of the mill since its inception. This was chosen by Agnes to be a religious symbol but still be sufficiently subtle not to offend anyone who did not share her own faith or her remarkable trust in Divine Providence.

[The chapel] was consecrated on September 22nd 1926 by Bishop Morrisroe of Achonry, and on the following day a colourful procession of bishops, priests and townspeople marched from the parish church to the new convent chapel. The chapel was the first one in Connacht to be consecrated within convent grounds.[2]

Agnes's final illness came in December 1931, but she survived until 21 April 1932. She died aged ninety, almost forty-one years to the day after she arrived in Foxford. Emma Sherry related the following regarding Agnes as her illness progressed:

Agnes Morrogh-Bernard had suffered with bad health for many years. She used to carry a folding walking chair with her and rested on it when the need arose. When the nuns were leaving Foxford a lot of things were left in the convent. Kevin, my late husband, brought the chair home with him. It is a constant reminder of the great lady and all she achieved.[3]

Bernadette Kimmerling, whose father, Jack Dorr, was a designer at the mill, related the following piece of history:

My mother was Bridie Clancy, from Limerick. She was a nurse and had trained at Barrington's Hospital there. She had come to Foxford as a private nurse to Agnes Morrogh-Bernard. She nursed Agnes when she was dying. Agnes couldn't eat anything, only sips of champagne. She had been instrumental in getting my Mother and Father together as a couple. After a fairly short courtship, they were married in August 1932 by Agnes's great friend Fr. Tom Finlay.[4]

Agnes did not live to see them married, having passed away the previous April. However, I am sure she was with them in spirit. A report of her passing was carried by the *Western People*:

One of the greatest Irish women of our century was laid to rest amidst every manifestation of deep and widespread regret at Foxford when the earth closed over the mortal remains of Rev. Mother Morrogh-Bernard, foundress of the Convent of Divine Providence and the Woollen Mills, which has earned worldwide fame. She was no longer a young nun when she came to Foxford yet few in the first flush of their youth could

The funeral of Agnes Morrogh-Bernard in Foxford, April 1932.

have manifested the same enthusiasm not alone in the religious order but in reconstructive social work in the poor districts in which she had come to make her home. She displayed the most amazing energy which had behind it the directing and controlling brain of a genius in organisation ... It was little wonder that the day was one of general mourning for the fine old lady who had dedicated over forty years of her life to gigantic enterprise and progress. She loved to talk of the magnificent factory, its unpretentious beginning, of the trouble she had in raising the funds necessary to launch the project even on a small scale. Five years ago her Order had the distinction of having the first church consecrated in Connaught within the convent grounds... [H]er funeral was of enormous size. The Convent chapel, spacious as it is, was altogether inadequate to accommodate the great gathering of people who came from far and near to bid farewell to the beloved nun.[5]

A large white crucifix in the grounds of the parish church in Foxford marks the burial plot for the Sisters of Charity, and the grave of Mother Agnes Morrogh-Bernard is a much visited site.

Agnes was predeceased ten days earlier by another founding member of the community, Sr Theckla, who was in her ninety-eighth year. Thus in a matter of ten days, two members of what was a bastion of the Foxford community were laid to rest.[6]

A few years later, in 1936, her friend Rev. Denis Gildea published her biography, entitled *Mother Mary Arsenius of Foxford*, with

Agnes's grave, in the nuns' plot in Foxford cemetery.

a foreword written by Bishop Morrisroe of Achonry, in whose diocese Agnes had worked so hard. The *Western People* hailed it:

> Of prime interest to the people of the West, and in particular to those of Ballaghaderreen, Foxford and Benada wherein the greater part of Mother Arsenius's life was spent. But it is of interest to the wide world over as the story of a great achievement by a frail and delicate woman possessed of a strong will, indomitable courage, and a never-failing confidence in the Providence of God.[7]

However, *The Tablet,* the British Catholic weekly newspaper, reveals that when the book arrived for review, the editorial staff were initially not too impressed with it and viewed it as:

> Another of the many edifying but monotonous lives of holy nuns whose lives and virtues are a common form.[8]

On further examination, however, they changed their mind:

> On looking into it we discovered our mistake. It proved the story of a nun who founded and controlled a successful woollen factory. This was something unexpected and unusual as could be imagined. And the nun in question was an equally unexpected and extraordinary woman.[9]

Mrs W. O'Brien pronounced that:

> A book like Father Gildea's is a treasure, to be read and taken up and studied over and over again, with new profit and enjoyment.[10]

Agnes was extraordinary, and a visionary into the bargain. She would have been proud of the accolades Gildea bestowed upon her in the book, but then she never looked for accolades, only fairness and equality for all in society.

The mill was going from strength to strength, as Nicola Depuis points out:

> At this time the success of the mill was at its peak, employing 230 workers. Agnes left behind her a successful industry which provided work, hope and dignity to generations of Foxford men and women.[11]

In 1933, a year after Agnes's death, an article in the *Western People*, entitled 'The West's Awake', written under the pseudonym 'One Who Knows', strongly proclaimed that Foxford was booming, and that the West was truly awake:

> Forty years ago it would have been hard to find a more backward town than Foxford; now it would be even harder to get one that is more progressive. What has caused this amazing transformation? The answer to this question is very important, because the problems overcome so successfully in this corner of Mayo, were precisely those which still confront scores of similar poverty stricken areas in so many parts of Ireland; how to replace backwardness, distress, and emigration by progress, prosperity and contentment. The solution of these problems in Foxford was due to the Sisters of Charity who began their labours there towards the end of the last century. When they arrived they found the whole district in a deplorable state. It was sunk in the deepest poverty; there was no industry; the emigration of the best youth was terribly heavy even for Mayo. The good nuns however, set to work and gradually changed all this. With tremendous zeal and heroic self-sacrifice they built

a small woollen factory. Formidable difficulties were present in the early days but by prayer and endeavour these were overcome. From humble beginnings the factory grew and prospered until now its employees number hundreds and it sends goods all over the civilised world. It goes without saying that the factory has checked emigration, for it gives regular work at good wages to young men and women who would otherwise have to leave their native soil.

In fact, so many and varied have the improvements been, that an exile returning today after an absence of forty years would hardly recognise the ramshackle town he left. The same spirit of preserving Christian solicitude is evident in every branch of social and cultural work. In education, in former times the facilities in Foxford were sadly deficient. Now there are commodious and up to date premises where every effort is made to promote the spiritual, mental and physical welfare of the pupils. The Sisters too are particularly keen on music and Irish studies. To further these they hold an annual Feis which is invariably a great success. It is also noteworthy that since their arrival many poor boys and girls have been able to enter the various professions, such as medicine, teaching and nursing. In the old days this was impossible. Finally in the midst of their manifold activities, the nuns have not forgotten the most important aspect of all – the spiritual needs of their employees. In most places, unfortunately, the factory system encourages, if it does not produce, moral and spiritual degradation. Not so in Foxford where the workers receive every incentive to practise their faith. As a result intemperance and kindred evils are happily rare. There is no need to enlarge further on Foxford's merits, though this would be easy. The main point is now what lessons do they teach us? Briefly, there are two lessons. The first is that the only solution of social and industrial problems is to be found in the general application of Christian principles as they have been applied in Foxford ... [T]he second lesson is that if all Irish towns developed their resources on the same lines as Foxford we should soon hear the last of the despondent wail that Ireland cannot supply her own manufactures. Thus may Foxford be held up as an example to the rest of Ireland, as a proof there is at least one place in the West not asleep, but very much awake – more so than any other town of its size in Ireland when it is a question of the things that really matter.[12]

In 2010 the Foxford Folklore Committee published a book entitled *Foxford Folklore – Changing Times: The 1938 Schools Collection Revisited*. The committee comprised Foxford Rural Social Scheme, Foxford Local History Group, Foxford Primary School, Foxford Secondary School and the interviewees. A number of the school children interviewed people who had worked in the mill, including Bridget Gallagher from Rinnanney, Foxford. Bridget worked in the woollen mill from 1945 to 1947. There were 250 people employed there at this time. Bridget gives the following account of her time in the mill:

> I was a weaver. I used to make cloth for the Mercy Sisters in Dublin and Roches Stores, also in Dublin. I used to see it written down. You couldn't get any of that as there was only enough made for them that were wanted. The nuns from Benada used to come in here to the mill and they used to sell rugs for two pounds and fifty shillings. The people used to buy them for weddings and one thing or another. The Super blanket was made out of softer wool and there was a ribbon along the side of them. They were the dearest blanket. There was a blanket with a row of blue and another bluer. That was that one, that was on the plain white blanket. There were also pram rugs. They were good and heavy for what they were. It was three and a half pounds. The tossles were solid and the little rabbit was on the front of it. Everything was first class; there were no seconds ...

[Y]ou [only] got seconds … if it was damaged, where a shuttle had opened or a thread had opened or something. Then all the blankets were brought down from a room called the burling room. They would put them across a big table. Then they would take all the knots out and put the thread back into it before it went down to the dye house. There they would put different colours harris tweeds, colours red, green and blue. It was very good. The wages were 12 shillings and 6 pence for a 48 hour week and you had to pay 2 shillings for your insurance out of that. There was a buzzer that would go off at ten to eight in the morning and then it would go off at 8 o'clock and when it would go off at 8 o'clock it would ring twice. You would know it was the last one. Then dinner time it would go and it would go off at 6 o'clock. That's how the people of the country would know the time too. It was the time of the war. Everyone knew the time. It could be heard in Swinford, Ballina. There was one hour for dinner; we used to have our dinner in town, in a house in town. Mine was up the street and this woman used to boil the kettle for four or five of us. It was one and six a week. The nuns could sack you there and then; they did, and they would. I came around by the cards and another time when I put my hand on the card, I was passing by the mules [and] a few of them broke. So she [a nun] was standing hiding above there. 'Come over here,' she said. 'Come over here. Was that you that came up there now?' I said 'Yes, Sister.' 'I am glad you told the truth,' she said, 'because I saw you.' She was watching me from the side. Oh, you couldn't be up to them. They would sack you to look around you that time. If you were a bad worker or timekeeper you were out. They had a hundred more to walk in your place. They didn't care, oh they didn't care. There was Sister Laurence and I liked Sister Lucia and I liked Sister Cannice. I didn't like Colm. I didn't know Sister Philomena. She was upstairs. She was supposed to be seen on the stairs [as a ghost]. Oh, she was a tall nun.[13]

Another employee in the mill was Margaret Maloney, formerly McTigue, who lived on Lower Main Street in the town. Margaret, who now lives in Stonehall, Foxford, worked in the mill from mid-1954 until 1962. She recalls:

> I worked weaving the material, using one loom; it was a very busy job. A Mr. Hamilton from Manchester arrived at the mill to carry out a time and motion study. The workers operated one loom but were told that each person could operate two looms. We thought this couldn't be done, but we were proved wrong. It could be done, thus creating a more efficient method. The wages were increased by one and a half. We were paid by cash. We queued up each Friday for our wages. Each person's wage was contained in a tin box with a number. The money was taken out of the box and the box returned to the office ready for the next week. Payment in cheque form was introduced at a later stage. If there was a disaster such as a flood, fire or famine abroad, the Red Cross would buy what was called a grey blanket. There would be a huge demand for those in cases like this.[14]

Margaret spoke of the co-operative store and its buzz of industry:

> At that time, a Mr Burke ran it. It was located at Providence Road. The bread I remember consisted mostly of batch loaves and nice bracks. I recall my mother coming home at Christmas-time telling us she had been paid a dividend of 2/6d. She was delighted with the money. The nuns also ran a dairy, where the library is now situated. Milk, that is what would be known now as full fat, was sold, and also skim milk, which was used to make bread, and perhaps puddings. The nuns were self-sufficient; they had a farm. Mr Sherlock was the steward who looked after it. Cattle, horses and poultry were reared. Vegetables were grown, with some exotic fruits tended to in the greenhouses. My father

was a blacksmith, and he used to shoe the horses. There were three forges in the town at the time. Goods were transported that time by horse and cart. Finished products would be taken to the train station, and materials for the mill would come by train and would be collected and taken to the mill, so the horse and cart was in constant use. The nuns gave people a great sense of self-worth. The town revolved around the mill, and it was part of everyday life. Sr Laurentius was very involved with the working of the mill. Sr Peter looked after the Pioneers and the sodalities. Sr Gregory was involved with the operas. Each nun had their own responsibility.[15]

She also spoke of the famous Corpus Christi procession that the nuns organised in the town:

The Corpus Christi procession in June was known far and wide. The nuns were responsible for organising it all. At that time, when a worker got married, there was the custom of going to the convent after the marriage ceremony and showing off the wedding dress. You would be taken into the parlour and the nuns would gather and admire the dress or costume on the day. It was nice, it made you feel good.[16]

Emma Sherry, too, spoke of the Corpus Christi procession, and the amount of work the nuns did in preparing for the event:

The men went out to Drummin Wood to gather moss. The moss would be twisted into ropes, and they would be draped from window to window in the town. Streamers and bunting bedecked the town. It was truly a spectacular sight.[17]

Imelda Turnbull recalled that:

A Corpus Christi procession in Foxford.

The men took it upon themselves to ensure that all the decorative bunting, streamers, etc., would be in place. The town was decorated from end to end. It was a gay, colourful, and spiritual procession. Music played a huge part in the procession, as music was such a big part of the community.[18]

Canon Michael Joyce, who is the current parish priest in Bohola, County Mayo, a few miles from Foxford, grew up very near the mill in the 1950s. The co-operative store was located on the same street as the Joyce household, on Providence Road. Joyce said:

The co-operative store was a hive of activity, which included a bakery and a chemist shop, where most things for the house and farm could be purchased. Mr O'Hanlon was the baker; the bread was sold on site and was also delivered to the local shops and to the homes throughout the hinterland. My father was the chemist there, and he dispensed what was required to the people. There was a dividend paid every Christmas to the workers, who of course purchased what they needed at the store. The dividend was 2/6d. The nuns had houses built for the workers in the mill, and they paid a weekly rent for them – 2/6d.[19]

Agnes's staunch friend Fr Finlay was the main force behind the setting up of the co-operative store. In her notes Agnes recorded:

> Fr. Tom Finlay had been the prime mover in establishing a co-operative society for the Mill hands in which they had taken shares. Finlay had borrowed money from the nuns to build the co-op. Mr Brosnan was brought in to run it.[20]

The co-operative store was a great success and it was to serve the workers well down through the years. It employed local workers, alleviating further the curse of poverty and unemployment.

Similar to Margaret Maloney's account of the industrial prowess of the nuns, Michael Joyce recalled that:

> The farm belonging to the nuns was run very efficiently. The convent was self-sufficient. I recall grapes, and other exotic fruits grown in the greenhouses. The nuns had two cars for their use, and a local man was employed as their driver.[21]

Housing for employees of the mill was provided by the nuns, and the workers paid a weekly rent for the house:

> The first of the houses built was on Providence Road and the present Main St, and later at Irishtown. The nuns gave the people the option to buy out the houses in the mid-1960s.[22]

In 1939 the Second World War broke out and dragged on until September 1945. Despite Ireland's neutrality, this war was to have an effect on the woollen mills. Frank Sherry recorded:

> Our biggest customer during the first year of the Emergency was the Controller of Army Stores. It was simple to deal with

his case: he wanted our total output and he got it. History records that an Irish brigade defeated a surprise attack clad only in their nightshirts but thanks to the Irish mills, there was no danger of our army being called on to prove they could do so again. One item in particular that we were called upon to supply about which we feel entitled to boast a bit, was the bunting in green, white and orange to make flags. This had never been made in the country before, and we feel proud that we were able to make the national flag in the height of the Emergency from Irish wool.[23]

He went on to describe the difficulties that both his mill and all the other Irish woollen mills experienced during the war: shortages of wool, dyes and oils so necessary to the processing.

He was a religious man and he placed his trust in the Lord adding a little prayer of his own: 'O Lord, don't send anything my way this day that you and I can't handle together.'[24]

Frank Sherry's prayers must have been heard, for he shepherded the mill through tough times and when he passed away in January 1949, glowing tributes were paid to him. *The Ballina Herald* carried the following report:

On Sunday there passed away in the person of Mr. Frank Sherry one of the oldest and most respected citizens. His life story since he came to Foxford fifty-seven years ago has been the development of the Providence Woollen Mills, of which he was manager during that time, in collaboration with the foundress of the convent and the factory, the late Mother Morrogh-Bernard, one of the most romantic and notable figures in the history of conventual life in Ireland. Mr Sherry, beginning as a young man fresh from Co. Tyrone in his native north, assisted in the building up not alone of the mills, but of the Foxford of our times. The name of the Foxford Mills has spread to the furthest ends of the world. Mr Sherry shared in the nurturing of the industry, the training of its hundreds of operatives, the extension of its buildings, which now cover many acres along the foaming waters of the Moy as it breaks over the rocks beneath the bridge, the setting up of a standard of quality and honest trading which has placed the mills on such a high plane in the industrial and commercial life of the country ... [T]he culture of the modern Foxford which has grown up round the Convent of Divine Providence carried on by the Sisters of Charity was reflected in the accomplishments of Mr. Sherry's family who were musicians of a high order and whose contributions on the concert platforms did so much some years ago to aid local and other charitable undertakings.[25]

In Frank Sherry's notes, recalled by Gildea, the following is recorded:

I came to Foxford in 1891 to start the mills as acting-manager. I soon discovered that though she [Agnes] was really very kind to me, the good of the mill was her paramount consideration. I did not then fully realize the importance of figures. Many a time her 'figuring' annoyed me; but in due course I saw the necessity not only of quality but also of quantities ... Time and again she put forward projects which I considered quite wrong and un-business-like. A period would then ensue during which no reference would be made to the matters discussed. During the interval she would have Masses celebrated and unceasing prayers offered. Then she would finally say something is telling me to do so-and-so. When that stage was reached, it was a case of going against my better judgment. Still I cannot recall a single instance in which she was deceived in the 'something that was telling her to do so-and-so'. I firmly believe she was inspired from on High.[26]

The war years, despite the shortages, brought a little excitement to Foxford. Noel Dorr served as Irish Ambassador to the United Nations in New York in 1980, as President of the United Nations Security Council between April 1981 and August 1982, Irish Ambassador in London from 1983 to 1987 and Secretary General at the Department of Foreign Affairs from 1987 to 1995. He grew up on Providence Road and in an interview in the *Western People*, he recalled that in 1944:

> I was playing near my own house when I saw a plane circling the town. It was clear that it was in trouble. It backed away from the town and came down in a bog a few miles away in Curradrish. Naturally enough we all trooped out to see this great bomber and the men who were in it. They had all escaped without injury and they were brought back to Johnny O'Donnell's, where Cruisers Pub is presently located. I remember the Americans had things like chewing gum – something we would never have seen. And then there was the plane itself, even though it was damaged beyond repair, there was material in the wreckage that still hadn't come to Ireland – plastic. People were making rings and other things from the plastic and passing them around. The Americans left Foxford that evening and were sent over the border into Northern Ireland. It was a really, really major event in our childhood.[27]

He spoke of the impact of the nuns on the town:

> The nuns were a very benevolent part of the town back then and they did huge good. They were a little bit autocratic and maybe that was not the best thing for Foxford. The town depended

on the nuns whereas in other places the nuns depended on the town. It was an unusual situation in Foxford.[28]

Autocratic or not, the nuns certainly did much good for the town and its people. Their arrival in the town heralded a new economic, spiritual, social and cultural epoch that would benefit many.

> On April 26 1942, the Golden Jubilee of the founding of the Woollen Mill was celebrated. A High Mass in thanksgiving was celebrated by the Bishop of Achonry, Dr. Morrisroe. Also a Pageant Play entitled 'Ways of Providence in Éire' was staged by the Mill's operatives. Part of both the Mass and Pageant was broadcast on the national radio station Radio Éireann. This meant that a large number of people throughout the country was able to listen to the proceedings.[29]

This is an extract from an article by Fr Ryan, a Jesuit who contributed to the *Irish Quarterly Review*:

> How dearly her memory is cherished was manifested in a thousand ways during the recent Jubilee celebrations. For in the decade since her death Providence Woollen Mills have continued to flourish, managed in her spirit by the Sisters and friends whom she trusted and loved. The workers now number more than 200, and the yearly wage bill is in the neighbourhood of £24,000. While towns and villages in other parts must rely on emigration, with its humiliations, its sorrows and its dangers, for the wherewithal to live, Foxford stands on its own feet. Its sons and daughters maintain themselves decently and religiously in their own country by the labour of their own hands. That is the heritage which Mother Morrogh-Bernard left them. Frank Sherry still stands in his old place at the wheel, ably assisted by his brother James; and the orchestra and choir,

under the masterly baton of Mr. O'Shaughnessy, make the finest compositions of music and song familiar on the Moy; and Kate Conroy, in her hospital home, points with pride to a telegram of congratulation from Pope Pius XII, received last year on the occasion of her own Golden Jubilee in the mill; and workers of incomparable skill, many now in the third generation, live honourably and well in their near dwellings, at peace with God and men; and tiny children and grandchildren, who appeared appropriately as angels, capturing all hearts in a scene of the recent Pageant, bring gleams of joy into the good Sisters' eyes, for in them lies the promise of a bright and perhaps, in the Providence of God, a yet more prosperous future.[30]

How proud Agnes would be of her enterprise if she could have read the praise of her and her industry. In September 1936 the *Irish Press* carried the following report:

> Mr Joseph Moorehouse, the proprietor of a jam factory at Leeds, which employs over 400 hands – many of them Irish – is on a motoring tour of the Free State. Since his previous visit, eight years ago, he has found evidence of great industrial progress. The Foxford Woollen Mills, he said, were a special revelation to him. It was wonderful to see there the manner in which the various processes of manufacture were carried out by highly-skilled workers, employed under conditions which were a credit to the management and the country.[31]

In September 1963 a Dublin correspondent reported in *The Connacht Sentinel:*

> It is good to know that there is at least one important manufacturing group preparing to meet the possible stresses

and strains of the Common Market. I refer to the Irish Wool Weavers' Co-operative Ltd. This body was set up recently to put the important tweed industry of Ireland on a footing which it is hoped will enable it to meet any strains which may arise from the Market. I notice that the famous Foxford Woollen Mills, an enterprise sponsored by a religious community and which met with very great success, will now be known as the Providence Woollen Manufactory. It hopes to increase its business and it appears to be the only tweed industry in the West which has joined the move. About 18,000,000 lbs. of wool are produced in this country annually, worth about £3,260,000. All Irish wool, unfortunately, is not suitable for the production of first-class goods but still much of it has been absorbed in the native industry and now that a new group has been formed on a co-operative basis it is believed that the work of all the mills as a group will expand … The new co-operative wants to get a better footing in the British, Dutch, French, German, Scandinavian and Austrian markets and it is said that there are prospects of getting into the Middle East and behind the Iron Curtain.[32]

Little did Agnes think that her fledgling enterprise would expand and attract buyers worldwide. In 1985 a Japanese delegation visited the mills:

A three-man Japanese delegation from the Christian Dior division of Kanebo Ltd. has been visiting the Foxford Woollen Mills this week. In recent times the Mills have been expanding their business in Japan.[33]

In the summer of 1987, however, Ireland's textile industry was in financial decline and Foxford wasn't immune. The mills went into receivership. This was a threat to the economic life of local families and of the town. In August 1987 a lockout took place at the woollen mill. Frankie Devaney, who began his working life as an employee at the mill and was later mill manager, recalls:

> I was offered a job by the Sisters of Charity in 1968 after the death of my Father at a relatively young age; he also had worked in the mill. I won a scholarship sponsored by ANCO, the precursor to FÁS, to the Scottish College of Textiles in Galashiels. I undertook training as a dyer of wool and associated fabrics and mill management. At the time there was a worldwide shortage of dyers. The process took three years. I was appointed mill manager in 1983, on the retirement of Seamus Sherry. I was familiar with every area of the day-to-day running of the mill. This included everything, starting with the raw material to the finished product. When I commenced work in 1968, there were around 150 employees in the factory, but by 1987 that number had been reduced to 83. There was a continuous sliding downwards through the 1970s and 1980s. I suppose the downward spiral of employment at the mill could be attributed to the fact that woollen products were in a very competitive market with synthetic products. The duvet had replaced the traditional blanket. The mill could not continue on this basis, so closure was inevitable. At the end we were asked to hand over our keys and go home, no more and no less. The thing seemed unreal and so final. The mill was closed and that was the end of the story. I had spent my whole life working there. We really had no idea that it was in such trouble. Looking back, the warning signs were there, but we always thought that it could hold out despite hearing rumours of financial trouble.[34]

A report in *The Sunday Business Post* read:

> During the first half of the 20th century, woollen mills had thrived on the huge demand for blankets and uniforms during

war-time. By the 1950s thousands were employed in the industry here. The establishment of the free market in the 1960s ended a protectionism that had been built into the industry in the early days of the Free State. In the 1980s the industry's decline was cemented with the advent of central heating. In 1987 Foxford Woollen Mills had made a loss of IR£110,000. The brand was dated; blankets were no longer a household necessity.[35]

Appointing a receiver to the mill must have been a very hard decision for the Sisters of Charity to make, owing to their intimate association with it. It was a decision that wasn't taken lightly, and in the end Rory Quinn, a Ballina-based accountant, was given the task. The Sisters of Charity wanted a firm commitment from whoever took over the mill that they would continue to run it and maintain as many jobs as possible. James Laffey pointed out that:

> One of the dangers was that someone could buy the factory, run it for a couple of months and then strip it down. The Sisters wanted to avoid that at all costs.[36]

Ivars Zauers was a designer at the mill. Having trained in the mills in Yorkshire, he started working in Foxford in 1963. He worked mainly on products for the export market. France, Germany and Italy were the three main countries that influenced the textile trade of the time, so Europe was a very important market. The Irish market at this time, the Lemass era, was very restricted.

> A special licence was necessary to import wool, which was required in the manufacturing of some products; the wool available here was not of the same standard. The amount

imported was restricted too. At least Lemass had the insight to see that the market had to be opened up, or the Irish trade was on a downward spiral.[37]

The solution for accessing the European market directly came about when:

> The Irish Wool Weavers' Co-operative was established in 1962 by Kurt Ticher and his son Tom in Dublin. The co-operative comprised a number of wool and textile mills, including Foxford. At this time, industrial expansion was vital to economic growth in Ireland, as up to this Ireland's market was constrained. The co-operative was Ireland's gateway into Europe. By joining together, there was a better chance for Foxford products to create a regular export market, rather than for a once-off consignment of goods. Working with European fashion consultants meant that Foxford products kept up with changing trends within the industry. Germany and Paris had the big trade shows, while Milan was the big make-up centre of the industry.[38]

Rory Quinn knew how crucial the European market was for the mill's products, and in this respect he knew he had to get workers into the mill in order for samples to be sent to the Paris trade show. If this didn't happen there would be no orders for the coming year. He asked some of the workers if they would be willing to come into the factory and in effect work for their social welfare benefit. The Department of Social Welfare wasn't too enamoured with this idea but eventually conceded and the workers came in and prepared samples for the trade show. Ivars Zauers recalled that:

> Paris furnished us with orders, and we had at last something

to work for. I think Foxford could be credited as being the first Industry where workers were allowed to work for unemployment benefit.[39]

With livelihoods in jeopardy, local business people came together to save the mill. Joe Queenan, a newly qualified accountant from Lahardane, a few miles outside Foxford, worked for Rory Quinn at this time. Together, they ran the factory from August 1987 until May 1988. While various investors were willing to buy the plant and move it outside the country, few showed any interest in saving it at its location in County Mayo. However, Joe Queenan knew the history of the woollen mills and decided he could not allow it to be uprooted and have its history disappear. He makes the point that:

> Agnes Morrogh-Bernard was an exceptional woman for her time. She was fifty years old when she founded the mill, which is probably the equivalent of seventy years old today, and a woman to boot. She was told to go home and say her prayers, but she didn't; she went out and made the factory happen.[40]

The rest is history. In 1988, at the age of twenty-seven and with no experience in textiles, Joe Queenan took over the running of the mill, with help from a small group of investors, a Business Expansion Scheme grant and financial aid from Enterprise Ireland. The *Mayo News* reported:

> The gradual decline of Ireland's once thriving textile industry has seen almost every working mill in the country close, one by one; each closure means the loss of livelihoods and the death of traditional craftsmanship as we know it in Ireland. Not so for Foxford Woollen Mills, established in 1891 by the

Convent of the Divine Providence. It seems that providence has stood to them as permanent closure is averted. Thanks to the commitment and dedication of local business people the mill survives once more. Local leaders shared the ambition to save the mills and with renewed investment jobs have been secured. The heritage and traditions of Foxford are set to continue well into the future.[41]

The Sunday Business Post carried an article in which Joe Queenan stated:

The range has to retain an innate Irishness, but also to appeal to younger people, who are far more design-aware as a result of travel and make-over TV shows. If I had been asked for advice by anyone thinking of buying the Mills in 1988, I would have told them to run a mile, but sometimes you do things in life, the logic of which doesn't stack up. Textile was a dirty word in the 1980s; the banks had lost a fortune on the textiles industry in the previous years and didn't want to know, but a few of us put a bid in and it was accepted. The Mill was the heart of Foxford and if it had been allowed to die the town would also have died. I began re-building the company by scaling it down. The business struggled through the nineties making some products it always had. The decision to change had to be made in order to become relevant to the market and to consumers or else go nowhere. It was a slow process, and if there's one thing I regret, it's that I didn't look for help and embrace change sooner. Having said that, people are surprised by the transformation of the company from a fuddy-duddy range to a bright new look. In 2002, designer Helen McAlinden began working with the mills in order to create a new up-dated Foxford brand. The outcome was a new-look range of rugs, blankets, throws, upholstered fabrics, furnishings and bed linen. The new products use new patterns and softer finishes as part of the Foxford Living range.[42]

Today there are fifty-two employees on the payroll at the mill. Queenan speaks with optimism of the industry:

> I was never more optimistic about the future of the mill. Business couldn't be better. We export to Japan, Scandinavia, UK, North America, Australia, and New Zealand. The market is export driven. Ongoing development of the brand, the sourcing and addition of more products, and investment in design and innovation is continuous all the time. The development of the export market is very important and is being worked on all the time. Ongoing training in weaving and finishing of products takes place in-house, and is also overseen by outside trainers.[43]

Evidence of the working mill is to be found in every feature displayed, and the historical is interwoven with the modern. But the wheels of this industry were not always as well oiled as they are today. Queenan points out:

> Things were very tough from 1988 up to 2000. I applied my own model of thought to the industry, and sometimes one doesn't know if this is the right thing to do at the time. A huge amount of hard work has gone into making the industry what it is today.[44]

Today, a seventy-seater restaurant is situated on the top floor, where a steady stream of people files in and out on a daily basis. It has a light, airy feel, with iconic Foxford items on display. The restaurant serves a wide array of local, seasonal produce. Joe Queenan emphasises the importance of this:

Here, as much as possible is home cooked and bought locally. Jams, chutneys, salad dressings are made in the restaurant kitchen. The same goes for Christmas cakes and puddings.[45]

Joe Queenan's thought process could be compared with that of Agnes as she stood by the banks of the Moy in desolated Foxford in 1891 and wondered if what she planned would come to fruition. All great doers have a sense of doubt at some stage – this is only human nature – but Agnes's and indeed Joe Queenan's faith in providence helped them to overcome any doubts and fears. Faith prevailed and providence did provide. Agnes would have been so proud when in 1995 the centenary celebrations of the Great Connaught Exhibition were held. She would never have envisaged that her industry would grow to such a size and become a worldwide brand.

Margaret Maloney was one of the people who took part in the centenary celebrations:

> A group of us boarded the train at Foxford and we went as far as Claremorris. On the return journey we re-enacted the events of 1895, depicting the mode of transport and costume of that time. I wore my grandmother's bonnet. The costumes were ordered in from Dublin, and it was a great occasion. The parade through the town was a truly spectacular one.[46]

The *Western People* carried the following report:

> The main event – the re-creation of the original exhibition – saw many of the traditional craft and cottage industries brought to life again. A train journey from Manulla (where people travelling on the Dublin to Westport train had to change), was re-enacted, tracing the journey of the famous visitors who

Re-enactment of the arrival of the looms to Foxford from Ballaghaderreen in 1892.

Paddy Naughton, the town crier, leading the Foxford Brass Band into town, heralding the arrival of the looms from Ballaghaderreen.

travelled to Foxford in 1895. Period dress of that time was worn, with a pageant and parade taking place through the town. The exhibition was opened by the Provincial Superior of the Irish Sisters of Charity, thus further enforcing the links which Foxford had with the order since the 1800s.[47]

Centenary celebrations at Foxford. Included are Margaret Maloney, her daughters Elizabeth and Louise, Sylvia Neary and the Lavin and Neary children. Photo courtesy of Margaret Maloney

Michael Conwell, Kitty Turnbull and Margaret Maloney at the centenary celebrations at Foxford Woollen Mills.
Photo courtesy of Margaret Maloney

This commemoration of the historic event, which was held to promote the fledgling mill in 1895, must have depicted just how much Agnes's industry had grown and developed over the course of one hundred years. As a result of a brave woman's courage and tenacity, a town and its people thrived.

The visitor centre was opened by Padraig Flynn on 1 May 1992. This was a milestone in the development of the mill, as the centre was the first of its kind in the country. Margaret Maloney worked on the committee, under the auspices of Foxford Resources, which eventually brought the visitor centre into being:

> I worked on the committee and it involved a lot of research. Researching the history of the mill, from its inception to the present day was quite an arduous task. However, it was well worth it. The visitor centre … was a brand new concept. Many, many people have passed through its doors, and it really tells the true story of Foxford in great detail.[48]

Frankie Devaney recalls that the idea of the visitor centre was the brainchild of Peter Hynes:

> The initial suggestion for the establishment of the visitor centre can be credited to the Mayo county manager, Peter Hynes. A native of Galway, he was an architect at the time with Mayo County Council, and he could see, with an outsider's perspective, that Foxford had something unique.[49]

Peter Hynes recalls that:

> Five hundred thousand pounds was the estimated cost of the project. One hundred and twenty thousand pounds had to be raised locally in order for the project to qualify for EU and

State grants. The fund-raising committee, namely, J. J. O'Hara, Michael Joyce, Brendan Forde, Fr Joe Caulfield and Martin Quinn, had to raise £40,000 through raffles and other means, while it was hoped that £80,000 could be acquired through local and regional companies. It was a daunting challenge. Joe Queenan, the manager of the mill, allowed rugs to be purchased at a discounted price of £10, and members of the fund-raising committee sold tickets for a raffle for the rugs on weekend nights in pubs across the county. Raffle cards with thirty lines at £1 a line were left into pubs during the week. They were collected and raffled at the weekend. The rugs were even transported to England and raffled there. A lot of other fund-raising activities were organised in Foxford. The last stage of the fund-raising drive was a draw of 1,000 tickets at £35 each. Each person who bought a ticket had the choice of a Foxford rug, duvet or personalised bath sheets, and one person would win a car. The draw was held towards the end of 1991 and the target of £40,000 had been reached.[50]

President Mary Robinson pictured at the visitor centre in 1992.

In the visitor centre the experience begins with a self-guided multimedia tour that covers the origins of the mill, the actual setting up of the industry and the pitfalls encountered, all the way up to the mill as it runs today:

A section of the crowd at the opening of the visitor centre. Second from the right in front is Evelyn Duggan RIP, sister of Lizzie Gaughan, who nursed Agnes during her illnesses down through the years.
Photo courtesy of Margaret Maloney

The history of the Woollen Mills is unfolded for the visitors through an ingenious three-dimensional audiovisual display presentation incorporating life-size models, including a talking head in authentic settings. The narrator of the story is Mayo-born Mick Lally, whose accent gives an authentic 'blas' to the proceedings.[51]

Sadly Mick Lally passed away in 2012. The tour takes about forty-five minutes and it is well worth seeing.

Another event that was held to celebrate the centenary was a competition for second-level schools. The theme was Local Development 1945–1995 and submissions were invited from secondary schools in the county. The *Mayo News* reported:

On Friday 2 February, 1996 teachers and organizers met with Dr Seamus Caulfield in attendance, to assess the progress to date. Throughout Mayo teams of students are busy gathering information on their local area, piecing together developments for submission of work by 29 March 1996. The organizers, Foxford Resources, Meitheal Mhaigheo, and sponsors Howley Distribution are eagerly awaiting submissions from schools as all indications point to very exciting and diverse projects.[52]

In April 1996 the *Western People* reported:

> It is highly encouraging to learn that one of our newest flagships, Foxford Woollen Mills Visitor Centre has won rave notices in a 32 county survey carried out last summer. One of the primary objectives was to gauge the level of satisfaction, and Foxford Visitor Centre staff were rated at 95% for efficiency while 85% was the nation's average. 52% reported that their expectations of the centre were exceeded, as against the national average of 29%. Value for money at the centre rated at 94%, 8% above the national average … the tourism potential is there.[53]

The Foxford story was not only recorded in print, but also gained worldwide attention when a documentary on the woollen mill was filmed by the national television station, RTÉ. The documentary entitled *The Nun and the Freemason* was produced and directed by Brendan Leeson and narrated by Augustine Martin. The Freemason referred to was of course Agnes's great friend and mentor John Charles Smith. The *Mayo News* reported:

> To a Mayo person watching the small screen during 'The Nun and the Freemason' it was a source of pride, but to have been a native of Foxford must have been sheer heaven.[54]

The account continued:

[Agnes] always said God's Providence was a rich bank, but people needed to help themselves. The Lord required the apostles to first produce the five loaves and two fishes before he worked his miracle. Agnes, in the course of her lifetime, transformed Foxford from another destitute, deprived Irish village into a centre not just of industry, but of music, culture, spirit and civic pride right up to her death in 1932.[55]

Agnes's trust in providence was proven a hundred fold over the years. Her unwavering faith and complete trust in a higher power helped her create a new epoch in her time.

The last of the Sisters of Charity left Foxford in the mid-nineties. There were scenes of sorrow as they bade farewell to the home they had known for many, many years. Eithne Brogan recalls that:

Frank McCullough making a presentation to the last of the Sisters of Charity to leave Foxford. Pictured are Margaret Maloney, Sylvia Neary, Sister Rosaleen, who taught in the commercial school, and Sister Elizabeth, Principal of the secondary school.
Photo courtesy of Margaret Maloney

Most of the Sisters of Charity went back to Dublin; some went to Kilkenny and Clarinbridge. If accommodation had been available for them, they might have stayed here in Foxford. They were part of the community for so long.[56]

Margaret Maloney had a similar view to Eithne Brogan regarding the nuns leaving Foxford. She recalled that many were very sad leaving the town and the community in which they had spent so many years:

If we had thought of it then, perhaps we could have formed a committee, and arranged for a house to be purchased for them. Hindsight is a great thing.[57]

Foxford Woollen Mills in 2014.

Above is the woollen mill of today, a place of industry, with cutting edge technology, combining the charm of the old world and the new. Foxford pieces are sold not only in Foxford but also in stores around Ireland and in selected retailers all over the world. They are available on the Internet at Foxford's online store. It is an inspirational place to visit. The vision that was created by Agnes all those years ago is a physical reality, standing as a testament to her audacity, tenacity and her belief in a higher power.

In her book *Nuns in Nineteenth-Century Ireland* Catriona Clear states:

> Nuns in nineteenth-century Ireland were, in one sense, very powerful women. They occupied a prestigious position in society, commanded a respect which was almost universal, and were free to devote themselves to work without biological interruptions or familial responsibilities. They were, on the other hand, the least powerful of all those who took vows in the Roman Catholic Church, being irrevocably barred from ordination, which was the gate to advancement and promotion in the modern Church. The unprecedented and disproportionately large growth in the numbers of women religious took place when the Roman Catholic Church was entrenching itself in all aspects of Irish life, and consolidating and centralising its power. The nineteenth-century was a transitional time in Irish society, with sweeping social, economic and demographic changes which affected women as much as everyone else.[58]

Providence Woollen Mills, St John's National School and the millrace in the early 1900s. The stone building in the background is the old corn store.
Photo courtesy of Mayo Library (the Wynne Collection)

From 1868 convents were eligible for financial aid on a capitation basis for orphanages and residential institutions that had training departments attached to them. The alacrity with which the provisions of the Industrial Schools Act were availed of by convents underlines the comparative ease of the nuns' assimilation into the enlarged functions of the secular state at this time. Clear writes:

> The Technical Instruction Act of 1889 (52 & 53 Vict. c. 76) which empowered local government bodies to grant-aid small industries from the rates was exploited to maximum advantage by religious communities. Small industries of one kind or another were operated by 10 per cent of convents by 1900.[59]

Nuns were seen as good managers, teachers and disciplinarians. Furthermore they were trusted in positions of authority:

> Nuns had a reputation of being good economic managers; this view was held by a witness to the 1887 inquiry into Dublin hospitals. The witness stated that because Jervis Street Hospital was run by nuns, it was run on an economic basis. As far as he was concerned, the enquiry needed no further explanation.[60]

Maria Luddy concurs with Clear regarding the status of nuns at this time in society:

> Nuns throughout the nineteenth century had a high social status. Their work in institutions and their own schemes of benevolence gave them a moral and spiritual authority which was unsurpassed by any other group of women in society.[61]

Enda McDonagh described Mother Arsenius as:

A feminist before her time, capable of meeting the men of church or state on equal terms, but also able to bring a feminine perspective to all her projects. She was non-sectarian in her religious disposition, and non-partisan in her politics. She was a woman of vision and of action, a woman of prayer and practicality. She brought hope to a destitute people not only for material improvement but also for a deeper communion with God in prayer and worship. Her life is an invitation to all concerned with survival and salvation in Mayo ... [H]er achievements survive her and are still evident in every corner of Foxford. The Woollen Mills, the schools, the interpretative centre, much of the housing in the town, the brass band and, latterly, Hope House all stand as a caution to any who may be tempted to give up the struggle for survival in Mayo.[62]

Here, Agnes's character is summed up succinctly: 'a feminist before her time'. And that is exactly what she was. She was fair, thorough in her dealings, and she didn't suffer fools gladly. Her main goal in life was in helping, caring and nurturing the body and the mind. She nurtured the body by the practicality of her plan; the means to earn a wage in order to afford food, clothing and a clean habitat for the people. The nurturing of the mind came in other forms – music, drama, prayer and social interaction. These were the things that mattered to her, in that she had the unique vision to see what would be important for her people in time to come. Most of all she gave people hope in a time when hope was so badly needed. People were enjoying a new sense of self-worth, seeing themselves earning a living and improving their lot slowly and steadily until her great plan became reality.

The writer John Banville stated:

I have always believed that local history is more important than national history. There should be an archive in every village, where stories such as the old man told me are recorded. Where life is fully and consciously lived in our own neighbourhood, we are cushioned a little from the impact of great far-off events which should be of only marginal concern to us.[63]

Certainly the local history of Foxford will be forever linked with Agnes Morrogh-Bernard, the nun who stood on the banks of the Moy and believed in the unbelievable, obtained the unobtainable, and delivered the unthinkable. Her belief in Providence was her bastion, her lifeline, her ship that would sail through the raging storm of life and reach the shore's safe haven. Gildea observes:

> If in God's good time the process of her beatification be initiated, Foxford and its factory will be standing monuments to prove the heroism of her trust in Divine Providence. The chimney shaft rising skywards symbolises the heavenliness of all her work. Like Gideon she spread out her fleece at the door of her tent. Certainly God bedewed it with bounteous moisture.[64]

Kitty Turnbull, a native of Clare, came to Foxford as a young teacher in 1948. She had tremendous admiration for the nuns and in particular for Agnes. Her daughter Imelda recalls:

> My mother often spoke of Mother Morrogh-Bernard and said if anybody should be canonised it should be her. She did so much good for the people and the community of Foxford at a time when things were very, very difficult.[65]

Let us hope the day of her canonisation will dawn in the not too distant future. Her goodness and selfless spirit will be an example for so many people.

Appendix I

Letter to Archbishop Walsh regarding Mary Aikenhead

THE SISTERS OF CHARITY,
MOUNT ST. ANNE'S, MILLTOWN,
Co. DUBLIN.

15 . 12 . 10

My dear Lord Archbishop
& revered Father

Our dear Mother
General showed me your
kind letter of 14th inst. &
the P.S. certainly means
a great deal!

We often heard of the
many long weary hours
& days you so generously
devoted to the "Cause" of the
Irish Martyrs & can fully
understand that you would

feel quite unequal
to go in for the same
ordeal again.

However, Mother General
can guarantee & I can
fully endorse it; that
nothing of the kind
now awaits you, in the
"Cause of our saintly &
revered Foundress, for
she will have everything
crisp & ready, so as to
save your Grace all
unnecessary trouble.

Besides, Friends in
Rome, who are used to

such things, have
promised their assistance
if we avail of their
present offer, to Mother
M. Berchmans Daly,
who asked me to
wire the word "Yes", on
16th at latest, if I may
do so?

We shall never get
such a chance again.

United by Mother
General in hoping
that your Grace will

see your way to
grant us this great
favor, which we ask
in your Jubilee Year.

I remain, with
much respect, your
devoted child in JC
Sr. M. Arsenius
(Morrogh Bernard)

Appendix 2

Decree issued by Bishop Donnelly

DOCUMENT 13

Copy of the Decree issued by Bishop Donnelly, V.G.
in the Archdiocese of Dublin in the absence of Archbishop
Walsh. A copy of the decree was sent to the Bishops of
the dioceses where Mother Mary Aikenhead had made
foundations. It was to be affixed to church doors from
1st to 30th September, 1912 inclusive.

TO THE CLERGY AND FAITHFUL OF THE DIOCESE OF DUBLIN

Whereas, in obedience to the injunctions of the
Apostolic see, it is necessary to collect all writings
attributed to the Servant of God, Mother Mary Augustine
Aikenhead, Foundress of the Religious Congregation of the
Irish Sisters of Charity, who died in the odour of
sanctity, at Our Lady's Mount, Harold's Cross, on July
22nd, 1858. If any of the faithful of this city or
Diocese have in their possession, or know that others
have in their possession, any manuscript or printed work,
whether autograph, or dictated, or composed by direction
of the aforesaid Servant of God, we order, under the
usual spiritual penalties, that within the space of
thirty days, to be counted from the 1st day of September,
1912, such persons present themselves before our Diocesan
Court and give such information regarding those works as
may secure their being duly lodged in Court. Those of
the faithful, who, from devotion to the Servant of God,
may wish to retain the original writings, may deposit in
their stead authenticated copies of the same.

We rest assured that all the faithful will gladly sec
the painstaking labours of the Holy See in the Cause
the Beatification and Canonization of the Afores
Servant of God.

Given at Dublin on this the 26th day of August, 1912.

```
        +        N. Donnelly, V.G.,
  SEAL              &c., &c.,
           President of the Diocesan Court.
```

Appendix 3

Letter regarding teacher training and education for all

6. XI. 10

THE SISTERS OF CHARITY
CONVENT OF DIVINE PROVIDENCE,
FOXFORD,
CO. MAYO,
IRELAND

My dear Lord Archbishop and revered Father,

Many years have passed, as you will see by Fr Finlay's Booklet, since you so kindly gave me permission to borrow the necessary money to start the Mill here. It will gratify your Grace to learn that the last of the 36 half yearly instalments to the C.D.B. of their Loan of £7000 was paid to them last week, which redeemed the Mortgage they had on Milltown since 1892. The enclosed cutting from the Cork Examiner of 29th Oct was sent to me. It shows the great success, which has been attained in our Schools in Cork.

Your Grace has done so much for education during the last 25 years, that it strikes me forcibly that in Dublin, where we have over 5000 children confided to our care in our Primary Schools, we ought to be able to bridge over the Gulf at present existing between Primary & University education and enable the poor man's child, to obtain the educational advantages so long denied to Catholics.

A simple plan, which would not be costly, could be devised, were our 3 largest C.N. Schools in Dublin to join, and give it a three years trial: Gardiner St, Stanhope St & King's Inns St could, without much extra difficulty, prepare some of their girls to go in for Matriculation in 1912, by starting now. To secure the success of this Scheme, they would require for the first few years, to restrict it to the Monitresses & Assistant Teachers, with very rare exceptions & carry it on apart from the ordinary work of these National Schools. The special instructions required should be given by good Grinders, well experienced in what is needed for Matriculation.

It would be very helpful to some of our young Teaching Sisters, were they to attend these Lectures — same as our Sisters in St Vincent's Hospital do — where they far surpassed the trained Nurses this year, at the Examinations for Certificates & Diplomas.

If you are at Milltown this week for the Profession, your Grace might see your way, to have a chat with our dear Mother General on this subject. She has a fine clear business head & would like to have the Sisters & Schools under her care doing good work. I remain, my dear Lord Archbishop & revered Father,

Your respectful & humble child in Xt. Agnes Morrogh Bernard

Appendix 4

Report of Henry Doran, CDB

CONGESTED DISTRICTS BOARD FOR IRELAND.

COUNTY OF MAYO—UNIONS OF BALLINA AND SWINFORD.

REPORT OF MR. DORAN, *Inspector.*

DISTRICT
OF
FOXFORD.
No. 42.

STATISTICAL TABLE.

Electoral Division	Area in Statute Acres	Poor Law Valuation	Number of Holdings valued under £4 Rent and Valuation	Number of Holdings in 1891	Population in 1891	Number of Families in 1891	Number of Families on Holdings valued at £4 Valuation	Number of Families holding under £4 Valuation	Number of Families having some other means	Number of Families which have no Cattle
		£								
Prehen,	4,525	1,194	20	233	1,945	255	140	77	120	
Toomore,	9,789	3,330	170	254	2,727	519	72	115	170	about
Callow,	7,674	1,908	138	215	1,897	357	178	28	100	120
Culdoo,	5,450	1,693	145	113	1,472	283	81	19	50	
TOTALS,	26,436	8,125	473	815	7,351	1,414	471	217	440	about 120

(1.) Whether inland or maritime.

The district is inland.

(2.) Average quantity of land cultivated on holdings at and under £4 valuation, under (a) oats, (b) potatoes, (c) meadow, (f) green crops.

There are about 4½ statute acres on an average cultivated on holdings at and under £4 in the following way:—

	acres
Oats	1 acre
Potatoes	1½ acres
Meadow, 1st Crop	1 acre
Green Crops,	none
Total	4½ acres

(3.) Extent of mountain or moor grazing, and whether possessed by tenants whether in connexion or otherwise.

The mountain grazing is chiefly occupied by tenants in connexion with their arable land. The cattle of the several owners run together. I could not ascertain the extent of such land, but it is not considerable, and is chiefly in Toomore Electoral Division and in the vicinity of Foxford.

(4.) Extent and description of land, if any, which could be profitably reclaimed and added to existing holdings.

Not much of the unreclaimed land is capable of profitable improvement. Some of it is too rocky, and there are tracts of wet deep bog that would not repay the outlay. A great deal of good, however, could be done by draining wet portions of holdings and reclaiming patches of cut-away bog and mountain, offering facilities for such work.

There would be about 1,500 acres of land of this class that would repay the cost of improvement.

(12.) Weaving, spinning, knitting, and sewing, whether used locally or sold, and where.

Some of the people in this district make frieze, flannel clothing, and blankets. All socks and stockings used are hand-knit. These things are made merely to supply family requirements, and not for sale.

(13.) Kelp-burning, and sale of seaweed.

The district is inland.

(14.) Sale of turf, nature and extent of bogs.

As a rule turf for fuel is easily procured. In some places there is an abundance of bog. There is not much turf sold.

(15.) Lobster fishing, number of men and boats employed.

The district is inland.

(16.) Sea fishing. Facilities for sale of fish, and number of men and boats solely employed in fishing.

The district is inland.

(17.) Number of men and boats employed in fishing, or carrying turf or seaweed. Classification of boats.

The district is inland.

(18.) Fish—whether consumed at home or sold.

The district is inland.

(19.) Extent of fish curing.

The district is inland.

(20.) Piers and Harbours, existing and suggested, and how far those existing are adapted to wants of district.

The district is inland.

(21.) Extent of salmon and freshwater fisheries. Number of men earning their livelihood therefrom.

A few men are employed at Salmon fishing (with nets) on the river Moy, which partly forms the boundary between Sraheen and Toomore.

(22.) Banks and Loan Funds.

There are no Loan Funds in the district. Banking accommodation is sufficient. There are Banks in Ballina and Swinford.

(23.) Mineral and other resources.

There are no mineral or other natural resources, that I am aware of.

(24.) Relative prevalence of cash or credit dealings, length of credit, interest charged, extent of barter, etc., etc.

Most of the people are more or less in debt to the shopkeepers and banks. In Ballina the shopkeepers do not give credit to the same extent as they did up to five or six years ago. Seeds and artificial manures are usually bought on credit
(See Report on the District of Swinford.)

(25.) Estimated cash receipts and expenditure of a family in ordinary circumstances.

The estimated *Cash* receipts and expenditure of a family of six persons, living on a holding of £4 valuation, are as follows:—

Receipts.	£	s.	d.	Expenditure.	£	s.	d.
Sale of 2 pigs	6	0	0	Indian meal for family			
„ Butter from 2 cows	3	10	0	„ „ pigs	5	10	0
„ Oats	3	10	0	„ „ poultry			
„ Straw or Hay	0	10	0	Oatmeal for family	0	10	0
„ Potatoes (when crop is good)	2	0	0	Flour, six 7st. bags, at 11/2s. each, or a less quantity when shop bread is available	3	12	0
„ Eggs from 20 hens	3	0	0	Shop bread	4	10	0
„ Chickens, 1 doz. at 4d. each	10	4	0	Tea and sugar	2	0	0
Savings of man for Lime working in England	5	0	0	American bacon	1	0	0
Average value of live stock sold	6	0	0	Tobacco for man	1	10	0
				Clothing—man, 1s., wife, 4ds., children, 10s.	7	0	0
				Candles, soap, oil, &c.	0	12	0
				Purchase of 2 young pigs	1	5	0
				„ 3 bags of artificial manure	1	10	0
				Rent of land and County Cess	4	4	0
				Salt fish and sundry requirements	1	0	0
	£32	14	0		£31	7	0

5

(30.) Character of the people for industry, etc., etc.

remuneration or of materially bettering their position by the improvement of their small holdings, they are too thriftless to attempt to work, and remain, winter after winter lounging idly about awaiting the time to return again to England.

(31.) Whether any organized effort has been made to develop the resources or improve the condition of the people; if so, by what means.

No effort has been made to improve the condition of the people, or develop the resources of this district.

(32.) Suggestions as to any possible method for improving the condition of the people in future.

The following are some of the methods I would suggest for improving the condition of the people as explained in my General Report dated the 30th April, 1892.:—

(1.) Improving the breeds of cattle, horses, donkeys, pigs and fowl. Special attention should be paid to fowl, and an effort made to induce the people to make the production of table fowl and eggs a special industry.

The circumstances of the small occupiers of land peculiarly fit them for the establishment of a fowl industry.

(2). Promoting better systems of agriculture, by appointing District Agriculturists, who would instruct the people in the most improved methods of farming, and offering prizes to persons who cultivate their farms in the best manner.

(3). By draining and reclaiming portions of the holdings under the supervision of the District Agriculturist.

(4) By migrating the large occupiers of land who have some capital and desire to migrate, and apportioning their land amongst the smaller occupiers.

(5). By establishing Technical Schools to educate children in branches of industrial work, which they can afterwards practise at home as a remunerative employment.

(6). By enforcing the Sanitary Laws and amending same, so as to compel the people to keep their homes and surroundings clean. This I would consider one of the most elevating influences that could be brought to bear upon them.

If cottage gardening be taken up by the Board, some means of educating the housewives how to cook the vegetables grown, must be in operation at the same time. This could best be done by sending a specially-trained woman round to the houses, who would there make up savoury dishes from the products of the garden, and let the people see what can be done in that way in their own homes.

Cottage gardening can be promoted through the agency of the District Agriculturist, and in the same way the planting of trees for shelter.

HENRY DORAN,
Inspector.

5th May, 1892.

To

The Congested Districts Board for Ireland.

Appendix 5

Census returns 1901 of the Irish Sisters of Charity, showing
Agnes Morrogh-Bernard as head of the house

Endnotes

Chapter 1 – Early Years

1. *The Freeman's Journal* (23 March 1841).
2. *The Kerryman* (25 December 1954).
3. Gildea, D., *Mother Mary Arsenius of Foxford* (Dublin, 1936), p. 11.
4. *Ibid.*
5. *The Cork Examiner* (7 May 1862).
6. *The Kerryman* (25 December 1954).
7. Gildea (1936), p. 32.
8. Clarke, F., 'Agnes Morrogh (Mother Mary Arsenius)', in Quinn, J. and McGuire, J. (eds), *Dictionary of Irish Biography*, vol. 1 (Cambridge, 2009), p. 491.
9. Cooke, C., *Mary Charles Walker: The Nun of Calabar* (Dublin, 1980), p. 29.
10. Clear, C., *Nuns in Nineteenth-Century Ireland* (Dublin, 1987), p. 102.
11. *The Tablet* (28 August 1915).
12. Depuis, N., *Mná Na hÉireann: Women Who Shaped Ireland* (Cork, 2009), pp. 13–14.
13. Peckham Magray, M., *The Transforming Power of the Nuns: Women, Religious, and Cultural Change in Ireland 1750–1900* (New York, 1998), p. 95.
14. Clarke (2009) p. 491.
15. McDonnell-Garvey, M., *The Ancient Territory of Sliabh Lugha Mid-Connacht* (Manorhamilton, 1995), p. 95.
16. Gildea (1936), p. 71.
17. Breathnach, C., *The Congested Districts Board of Ireland 1891–1923* (Dublin, 2005), p. 57.
18. Memoirs of Agnes Morrogh-Bernard, 22 October 1889 (copy, Foxford, unpublished).
19. Clancy, P., *A Journey of Mercy from Birth to Re-Birth* (Swinford, 1994), pp. 143–4.
20. Manning, M., *James Dillon: A Biography* (Dublin, 1999), pp. 9–10.
21. Gildea (1936), p. 87.
22. *The Daily Chronicle* (13 February 1897).
23. Moore, M., 'A New Woman's Work in the West of Ireland', in *Catholic*

World, vol. 64, no. 1897, pp. 451–8.

24. Williams, W. H. A., *Landscape, Tourism, and the Irish Character: British Travel Writers in Pre-Famine Ireland, 1750–1850* (Wisconsin, 2008), p. 92.

25. RSCG/H26/449, p. 51.

26. Reid, T., *Travels in Ireland in the Year 1822: Exhibiting Brief Sketches of the Moral, Physical, and Political State of the Country: with Reflections on the Best Means of Improving Its Condition* (London, 1823), p. 215.

27. Maguire, C., 'The Health of the Irish People', in *Studies* (1913) vol. 5, pp. 823–34.

28. *The Weekly Irish Times* (31 December 1904).

29. Laffey, J., *Foxford Through the Arches of Time* (Westport, 2003), p. 17.

30. O'Grada, C., *Ireland's Great Famine: Interdisciplinary Perspectives* (Dublin, 2006), p. 77.

31. McDonagh, E. (ed.), *Survival or Salvation: A Second Mayo Book of Theology* (Dublin, 1994), p. 87.

32. *Ibid.*

33. RSCG/H13/91.

34. Peckham Magray (1998), p. 98.

35. Clear (1987), p. 116.

Chapter 2 – Foxford

1. Heaney, M. J., *Galway and Mayo Families* (unpublished, *c.* 1984), p. 12.

2. Laffey (2003), p. 8.

3. Bingham-Daly, T., *The Mayo Binghams* (Bishop Auckland, 1997), p. 83.

4. Dun, F., *Landlords and Tenants in Ireland* (London, 1881), p. 223.

5. Lenihan, P., *Consolidating Conquest: Ireland 1603–1727* (Harlow, 2008), pp. 138–9.

6. Micks, W. L., *An Account of the Congested Districts Board for Ireland* (Dublin, 1925), pp. 11–12.

7. Crowley, J. *et al.*, *Atlas of the Great Irish Famine 1845–52* (Cork, 2012), p. 281.

8. Woodham-Smith, C., *The Great Hunger* (London, 1991), p. 33.

9. Mokyr, J., *Why Ireland Starved: A Quantitative and Analytical History of the Irish Economy, 1800–1850* (London, 1985), p. 294.

10. Breathnach (2005), p. 110.

11. Kinealy, C., *This Great Calamity: The Irish Famine 1845–52* (Dublin, 1994), p. 345.

12. Bardon, J., *A History of Ireland in 250 Episodes* (Dublin, 2008), p. 369.

13. The Poor Relief Ireland Act 1838 (1 & 2 Vict. c. 56).

14. Henry, C., 'The Swinford Union Poor Law Administration', in Garavin, J. (ed.), *The Mayo Association Year Book 1998* (Dublin, 1998), pp. 27–8.

15. *The Connaught Ranger* (26 August 1846).
16. George Vaughan Jackson to the Chief Secretary, 8 November 1845, in Swords, L., *In Their Own Words: The Famine in North Connacht 1845–1849* (The Columba Press, Dublin, 1999).
17. Greer, J., *The Windings of the Moy* (Dublin, 1924), pp. 165–7.
18. Fox, A. J., Dublin Mansion House Committee Report on the Condition of the Peasantry of the County of Mayo in 1880, in *The Irish Crisis of 1879–80: Proceedings of the Dublin Mansion House Relief Committee 1880* (Dublin, 1881), pp. 105–22.
19. *Ibid.*
20. Third Report of Dr. Sigerson and Dr. Kenny, July 16 1880, in *The Irish Crisis of 1879–80: Proceedings of the Dublin Mansion House Relief Committee 1880* (Dublin, 1881), p. 141.
21. Finlay, T. A., 'Foxford Then and Now', in *New Ireland Review*, vol. xiv (September 1900), pp. 5–6.
22. Micks (1925), p. 10.
23. Coogan, T. P., *The Famine Plot: England's role in Ireland's Greatest Tragedy* (New York, 2012), p. 22.
24. Biggs-Davison, J., *George Wyndham: A Study in Toryism* (London, 1951), pp. 116–17.
25. Ardagh, J., *Ireland and the Irish: Portrait of a Changing Society* (London, 1994), p. 22.
26. O'Hara, B., *Davitt* (Castlebar, 2006), p. 40.
27. Davitt, M., *Jottings in Solitary* and edited by C. King (Dublin, 2003), p. 8.
28. O'Hara (2006), p. 40.
29. *The Connaught Telegraph* (8 May 1880).
30. Campbell, F., *Nationalist Politics in the West of Ireland 1891–1921* (New York, 2005), pp. 28–9.
31. Laffey (2003), p. 12.

Chapter 3 – The Establishment of the Foxford Woollen Mills

1. Memoirs of Agnes Morrogh-Bernard, March 1891 (copy, Foxford, unpublished).
2. Preston, W., 'Life and Writings of William Preston 1753–1807', in *Studies*, vol. 31 (1945), p. 383.
3. Aguinis, M., *Admiral William Brown: Liberator of the South Atlantic* (Foxford, 2006), p. 24.
4. Finlay, T. A., *Foxford and the Providence Woollen Mills* (Dublin, 1940), pp. 19, 21.
5. Gildea (1936) p. 98.
6. Butler, M. M., *A Candle was Lit: The Life of Mother Mary Aikenhead* (Dublin, 1953), pp. 172–3.

7. *Morning Post* (31 October 1896).
8. *Belfast News Letter* (15 March 1892).
9. *Ibid.*
10. Quigley, A. A., *Green Is My Sky* (Dublin, 1983), pp. 34–5.
11. *Ibid.*
12. Laffey (2003), pp. 166–7.
13. See Chapter 5 for a full account of the CDB.
14. Memoirs of Agnes Morrogh-Bernard, September 1891 (copy, Foxford, unpublished).
15. *Ibid.*, 5 March 1892.
16. *Ibid.*, April 1892.
17. Agnes Morrogh-Bernard to Mrs Margison (28 October 1892), RSCG/H26/1.
18. Congested Districts Board (CDB), First Annual Report (31 December 1892), p. 20.
19. CDB, Second Annual Report (31 December 1893), p. 27.
20. *Ibid.*
21. Laffey (2003), p. 18.
22. *Evening Telegraph* (6 April 1892).
23. Finlay (1940) p. 23.
24. Laffey (2003), p. 19.
25. *The Freeman's Journal* (4 May 1893).
26. Meehan, R., *The Story of Mayo* (Castlebar, 2003), p. 340.
27. Butler (1953), p. 173.
28. *The Freeman's Journal* (20 December 1892).
29. Interview with Frankie Devaney (14 November 2013).
30. *The Freeman's Journal* (4 May 1893).
31. Memoirs of Agnes Morrogh-Bernard, 1891 (copy, Foxford, unpublished).
32. *The Freeman's Journal* (16 November 1893).
33. *Ibid.*
34. Interview with Eithne Brogan (20 March 2014).
35. *The Freeman's Journal* (13 August 1894).
36. *Ibid.*
37. *The Irish Times* (28 August 1895).
38. Memoirs of Agnes Morrogh-Bernard, May 1895 (copy, Foxford, unpublished).
39. *The Freeman's Journal* (14 January 1895).
40. Laffey (2003), p. 19.
41. *The Irish Times* (20 September 1895).
42. Letter of Lady Winifred Arran in *The Irish Times* (26 February 1896).
43. RSCG/H/26/449, p. 65.
44. *Mayo News* (24 April 1897).

45. Swords, L., *A Dominant Church: The Diocese of Achonry 1818–1960* (Dublin, 2004), pp. 319–20.
46. *Morning Post* (31 October 1896).
47. *Ballina Herald* (30 January 1896).
48. *The Irish Homestead* (1 February 1896).
49. Memoirs of Agnes Morrogh-Bernard, January 1896 (copy, Foxford, unpublished).
50. *The Educational Times* (April 1899).
51. O'Riordan, M., *Catholicity and Progress in Ireland* (London, 1906), pp. 409–10.
52. *Ibid.* pp. 410–12.
53. Greer (1924), p. 169.
54. *Daily Chronicle* (22 February 1897).
55. Beuner, C. S., 'Coping with Want in the West: A Permanent Local Remedy, What An Irish Nun Has Done', in *New Zealand Tablet*, vol. xxvi (15 July 1898), p. 27.
56. *Ibid.*
57. Depuis (2009), p. 184.
58. *The Freeman's Journal* (14 September 1895).
59. *The Weekly Irish Times* (5 August 1922).

Chapter 4 – The Congested Districts Board

1. Curtis, L. P., *Coercion and Conciliation in Ireland: A study in Conservative Unionism* (New Jersey, 1963), p. 358.
2. Hickey, D. J., and Doherty, J. E., *A Dictionary of Irish History* (Dublin, 1980), p. 87.
3. Bull, P., *Land, Politics, and Nationalism: A Study of the Irish Land Question* (Dublin, 1996), p. 67.
4. *Ibid.*
5. King, C. *et al.*, *The West of Ireland: New Perspectives on the Nineteenth Century* (Dublin, 2011), pp. 170–1.
6. CDB, First Annual Report (Dublin, 1892), p. 1.
7. Bielenberg, A., and Breathnach, C., *Family income and expenditure in the West of Ireland: the evidence from the Baseline Reports of the Congested Districts Board* (Cork, 2000), p. 1.
8. Shannon, C. B., *Arthur J. Balfour and Ireland 1874–1922* (Washington, 1988), p. 54.
9. *Ibid.*
10. Breathnach (2005), p. 11.
11. Irish Church Act 1869 (32 & 33 Vict. c. 42).
12. Comerford, R. V., 'Gladstone's First Irish Enterprise 1864–1870', in Vaughan, W. E. and Moody, T. W. (eds), *A New History of Ireland: Ireland*

under the Union 1801–1870, vol. v (Oxford, 1989), pp. 431–49.

13. CDB, First Annual Report (Dublin, 1892), p. 4.
14. TNA (*Kew*), Series T/91.
15. CDB, First Annual Report (Dublin, 1892), p. 4.
16. Sea and Coast Fisheries Fund (Ireland) Act 1884 (47 & 48 Vict. c. 21).
17. CDB, First Annual Report (Dublin,1892), pp. 4–5.
18. Ferriter, D., *The Transformation of Ireland 1900–2000* (London, 2004), pp. 62–3.
19. Land Law Ireland Act 1881 (33 & 34 Vict. c. 46).
20. The Purchase of Land (Ireland) Act 1885 (48 & 49 Vict. c. 73).
21. Ó Broin, L., *The Chief Secretary: Augustine Birrell in Ireland* (London, 1969), pp. 20–4.
22. O'Hara (2006), p. 85.
23. Dooley, T., *The Land for the People: The Land Question in Independent Ireland* (Dublin, 2004), p. 19.
24. Nolan, R., *Within the Mullet* (Galway, 2000), p. 123.
25. Dooley, T., *The Big Houses and Landed Estates of Ireland: A Research Guide* (Dublin, 2007), p. 62.
26. CDB, First Annual Report (Dublin, 1892), p. 22.
27. *Ibid.*, p. 1.
28. King (2011), p. 171.
29. Hayes, A. and Urquart, D., *The Irish Women's History Reader* (London, 2001), p. 211.
30. CDB, Eighth Annual Report (Dublin, 1899) pp. 27–9.
31. Micks (1925), p. 179.
32. Hinkson, P., *Seventy Years Young: Memories of Elizabeth Countess of Fingall* (Dublin, 1991), pp. 281–2.
33. Meehan (2003), p. 68.
34. McCarthy-Filgate, W. T. M., *Irish Rural Life and Industry with Suggestions for the Future* (Dublin, 1907), p. 280.
35. Davitt, M., *The Fall of Feudalism in Ireland* (London, 1904), pp. 663–4.
36. Breathnach (2005), p. 170.
37. Dunleavy, J., 'Keir Hardie's Visit to Mayo in 1906', in *Journal of the Westport Historical Society,* vol. 10, no. 1 (1990), pp. 79, 81.
38. *Ibid.*, p. 81.
39. Lee, J., *The Modernisation of Irish Society 1848–1918* (Dublin, 1973), p. 129.
40. Shannon (1988), p. 56.
41. *Irish Daily Independent* (25 January 1895).
42. Travers, P., *Settlements and Divisions Ireland 1870–1922* (Dublin, 1988), p. 59.
43. O'Grada, C., *Ireland: A New Economic History 1780–1939* (New York, 1995), p. 264.

44. Maume, P., *The Long Gestation: Irish Nationalist Life 1891–1918* (Dublin, 1999), p. 18.
45. *Ibid.*, p. 269.
46. West, T., *Horace Plunkett: Co-operation and Politics: An Irish Biography* (Gerrard's Cross, 1986), pp. 32–3.
47. Nelson, B., *Irish Nationalists and the Making of the Irish Race* (Princeton, 2012), p. 154.
48. Daly, M. E., *The First Department: A History of the Department of Agriculture* (Dublin, 2002), p. 36.
49. West (1986), p. 24.
50. Ferriter (2004), p. 67.
51. Matthews, P. J., *Revival: The Abbey Theatre, Sinn Féin, the Gaelic League and the Co-operative Movement* (Cork, 2003), p. 67.
52. Tuke, J. H., *Irish Distress and Its Remedies: A Visit to Donegal and Connaught, February, March and April 1880* (Michigan, 1880), p. 124.
53. Tuke, J. H., *Ought Emigration from Ireland to Be Assisted?* (London, 1882), p. 175.
54. Fry, E., *James Hack Tuke: A Memoir* (London, 1899), p. 206.
55. Jordan, D. E., *Land and Popular Politics in Ireland: County Mayo from the Plantation to the Land War* (Cambridge, 1994), pp. 108–10.
56. *Illustrated London News* (13 October 1849).
57. Madden, F. J. M., *Teach Yourself the History of Ireland* (London, 2005), p. 76.

Chapter 5 – Agnes the Fearless Campaigner

1. Agnes Morrogh-Bernard to Henry Doran, RSCG/H26/041.
2. Henry Doran to Agnes Morrogh-Bernard, RSCG/H26/041.
3. Agnes Morrogh-Bernard to John Dillon (8 December 1918), PRO, TCD 6859/60/398.
4. Agnes Morrogh-Bernard to John Dillon (8 December 1919), PRO, TCD 6859/60/398.
5. Agnes Morrogh-Bernard to John Dillon (8 November 1923), PRO, TCD 6859/60/405.
6. *The Connaught Telegraph* (23 September 1911).
7. Memoirs of Agnes Morrogh-Bernard, November 1896 (copy, Foxford, unpublished).
8. *Ibid.*
9. *Ibid.*
10. Kernaghan, P., *Watching for Daybreak: A History of St Matthew's Parish, Belfast* (Belfast, 2000), pp. 20–1.
11. Lysaght, C., *Great Irish Lives* (London, 2008), pp. 155–6.
12. Annals of Foxford, RSCG/H/21, pp. 63, 75.

13. Swords (2004), p. 348.
14. Joyce, B., *Agnes Morrogh-Bernard 1842–1932, Foundress of the Foxford Woollen Mills* (Foxford, 1992), p. 26.
15. Agnes Morrogh-Bernard to Archbishop Walsh (8 October 1912), RSCG/H26/181-274.
16. Gildea (1936), p. 159.
17. *Ibid.*
18. *Ibid.*, p. 162.
19. Cardinal Moran to Mother Gertrude (20 December 1909), RSCG/2/6.
20. Gildea (1936), pp. 166–7.
21. *Ibid.*, pp. 167–8.
22. *Ibid.*, p. 168.
23. Prince, J. F. T., 'Comprehensive Congregation', in *The Catholic Herald* (18 July 1958).
24. www.rsccaritas.ie/rscnews/487-history-of-the-cause (accessed 22 January 2014).
25. Interview with Sister Monica Byrne (23 January 2014), RSCG.
26. Interview with Sister Marie O'Leary (11 April 2014), RSCG.
27. Cooke (1980), pp. 16, 20–2, 25.
28. *Ibid.*, p. 28.
29. *Ibid.*, p. 31.
30. *Ibid.*
31. Leen, E., 'A Great Irish Missionary: Bishop Joseph Shanahan CSSp.', in *Studies* (June 1944), vol. 33, pp. 145–57.
32. Cooke (1980), pp. 33–4.
33. Mother Agnes Gertrude to Bishop Shanahan (25 April, 1915), RSCG/ H26/191.
34. Cooke (1980) pp. 37–8.
35. *Ibid.*, p. 34.
36. Memoirs of Agnes Morrogh-Bernard, 1919 (copy, Foxford, unpublished).
37. Cooke (1980), p. 38.
38. Mother Agnes Gertrude to Agnes Morrogh-Bernard (*c.* 1919/20), in Cooke (1980), pp. 38–9.
39. *Ibid.*
40. Bishop Shanahan to Agnes Morrogh-Bernard (4 March 1926), RSCG/ H26/288.
41. Bishop Shanahan to Mary Martin (16 June 1923), Medical Missionaries of Mary Archives, CO/1/43.
42. Smyth, I., 'A Dream to Follow', in *Healing and Development Yearbook 2001* (Dublin, 2001), p. 24.
43. Hackett, R. I. J., *Religion in Calabar: The Religious Life and History of a Nigerian Town* (Berlin, 1988), p. 78.

44. Forristal, D., *The Second Burial of Bishop Shanahan* (Dublin, 1990), p. 173.
45. Agnes Morrogh-Bernard to Mary Charles Walker (*c.* 1923/24), RSCG/ H26/336.
46. Mary Charles Walker to Agnes Morrogh-Bernard (*c.* 1923), RSCG/ H26/336.
47. *Ibid.*
48. Agnes Morrogh-Bernard to Mary Charles Walker (12 June 1924), RSCG/H26/336.
49. McDonagh (1994), pp. 86–7.
50. Clancy (1994), p. 142.

Chapter 6 – Agnes and the Politics of the Time

1. Agnes Morrogh-Bernard to Bishop Lyster (24, 27, 28 July 1892), RSCG/ H26/449.
2. McDonagh (1994), p. 90.
3. *Ibid.*
4. Swords (2004), p. 301.
5. Agnes Morrogh-Bernard to Bishop Lyster (*c.* 1891), RSCG/H26/449.
6. Memoirs of Agnes Morrogh-Bernard, September 1895 (copy, Foxford, unpublished).
7. Duffy, E., 'Mother Arsenius and the Eye of Providence', in McDonagh, E. (ed.), *Survival or Salvation: A Second Mayo Book of Theology* (Dublin, 1994), p. 90.
8. Laffey (2003), p. 102.
9. *Ibid.*
10. Gregory, A. and Paseta, S., *Ireland and the Great War: A War to Unite Us All* (Manchester, 2002), p. 78.
11. Purdon, E., *The Irish Civil War 1922–1923* (Dublin, 2000), p. 69.
12. Horace Plunkett to Agnes Morrogh-Bernard (9 September 1920), RSCG/H26/170.
13. *Irish Independent* (25 May 1921).
14. Laffey (2003), p. 112.
15. *Western People* (November 1921).
16. Laffey (2003), p. 116.
17. Quigley (1983), p. 40.
18. *Ibid.*
19. Gildea (1936), pp. 178–9.
20. Swords, (2004), RSCG/H/26/178.
21. Quigley (1983), p. 39.
22. Hinkson (1991), p. 399.
23. *Ibid.*
24. *The Irish Times* (15 July 1922).

25. *Western People* (29 July 1922).
26. *The Irish Times* (26 July 1922).
27. Agnes Morrogh-Bernard to Mother General (5 July 1922), RSCG/ H26/87.
28. *Irish Independent* (27 July 1922).
29. *The Weekly Irish Times* (5 August 1922).
30. Collins, M., *The Path to Freedom* (Cork, 1995), pp. 107–8, 111–12.
31. Laffey (2003), p. 115.
32. *Western People* (29 January 1997).
33. Beattie, J., *Foxford Folklore – Changing Times: The 1938 Schools Collection Revisited* (Foxford, 2010), p. 28.
34. Interview with Ivars Zauers (7 May 2014).
35. Purdon (2000), pp. 57–8.
36. McCaffrey, C., *In Search of Ireland's Heroes* (Chicago, 2006), p. 242.

Chapter 7 – Success

1. CDB, Report of visit of Mr. W. J. D. Walker to W. L. Micks, RSCG/ H26/O32.
2. CDB, Second Annual Report (1893), p. 28.
3. *Ibid.*, p. 26.
4. Memoirs of Agnes Morrogh-Bernard, August 1896 (copy, Foxford, unpublished).
5. *Pudsey District Advertiser* (20 August 1896).
6. Memoirs of Agnes Morrogh-Bernard, 29 August 1896 (copy, Foxford, unpublished).
7. *The Connaught Telegraph* (15 August 1896).
8. Hinkson (1991), p. 249.
9. Helland, J., 'A Delightful Change of Fashion: Fair Trade, Cottage Craft, and Tweed in Late Nineteenth-Century Ireland', in *The Canadian Journal of Irish Studies*, vol. 36, no. 2 (2010), p. 42.
10. www.stanhopesecondary.ie/our-school/history (accessed 4 January 2014).
11. *The Freeman's Journal* (20 December 1892).
12. *Belfast News Letter* (5 April 1898).
13. *Western People* (22 February 1896).
14. Helland, J., (2010), p. 37.
15. *Ibid.*, pp. 40–1.
16. *Evening Telegraph* (6 April 1892).
17. Mitchell, G., *Deeds Not Words: The Life and Work of Muriel Gahan* (Dublin, 1997), p. 51.
18. *Ibid.*, p. 54.
19. Cruise-O'Brien, M., *The Same Age As The State* (Dublin, 2003), p. 178.
20. Swords (2004), p. 322.

21. Memoirs of Agnes Morrogh-Bernard, 1 November 1910 (copy, Foxford, unpublished).
22. CDB, Nineteenth Annual Report (1911), p. 35.
23. Interview with Imelda Turnbull (25 January 2014).
24. *Ibid.*
25. Interview with Bernadette Kimmerling (8 August 2012).
26. Meehan (2003), p. 341.
27. CDB, Ninth Annual Report (1900), p. 41.
28. *London Daily News* (24 April 1900).
29. Finlay (1940), pp. 11, 13.

Chapter 8 – Famous Visitors to the Mill

1. Campbell Gordon Aberdeen, J., and Gordon Aberdeen, I., *We Twa: Reminiscences of Lord and Lady Aberdeen*, vol. I (London, 1925), p. 336.
2. Memoirs of Agnes Morrogh-Bernard, 14 July 1893 (copy, Foxford, unpublished).
3. *Western People* (15 July 1893).
4. Pentland, M., *A Bonnie Fetcher* (London, 1952), p. 60.
5. *Ibid.*, p. 103.
6. Keane, M., *Ishbel: Lady Aberdeen in Ireland* (Newtownards, 1999), p. 66.
7. Pentland (1952), pp. 102–3.
8. *Ibid.*, p. 69.
9. *Huddersfield Chronicle* (3 June 1893).
10. Stephens, D., 'Davy's Kolumn', in *Kingstown Monthly* (July 1893).
11. *Western People* (15 July 1893).
12. Keane (1999), p. 49.
13. Hinkson (1991), 274–5.
14. Gatty, C. T., *Recognita* (London, 1917), p. 159.
15. Quigley (1983), pp. 46–7.
16. *The Freeman's Journal* (13 April 1898).
17. Michael Davitt to William O'Brien (*c.* 1898), NLI 914/1044.
18. *Western People* (7 September 1935).
19. *Western People* (23 July 1938).
20. Sullivan, M., *Mary Robinson: The Life and Times of an Irish Liberal* (Dublin, 1993), p. 8.
21. *Ibid.*, p. 9.

Chapter 9 – Challenge and Achievement

1. Masahiko, Y., 'George A. Birmingham. *General John Regan*: A Hearty Wish for Reconciliation between every Human Being', in *JWHS*, vol. 30, (Westport, 2012), pp. 9–10.

2. G. A. Birmingham, *Hyacinth* (London, 1906), pp 239–40.
3. *Ibid.*, pp. 277–9.
4. *Ibid.*, p. 290.
5. *Mayo News* (17 March 1906).
6. *Ibid.*
7. *The Catholic Times* (June 1906).
8. Mrs W. M. O'Brien, 'Mother Arsenius of Foxford by Fr Denis Gildea' in *The Irish Monthly*, vol. 64 (760) (Irish Jesuit Province, 1936), p. 710.
9. G. A. Birmingham, *Benedict Kavanagh* (London, 1907), p. v.
10. Peter Murray, 'Novels, Nuns and the Revival of Irish Industries: The Rector of Westport and the Foxford Woollen Mill 1905–1907', in *JWHS* vol. 8 (Westport, 1988), pp. 89–90.
11. *Ibid.*
12. *Ibid.*
13. Masahiko (2012), pp. 9–10.
14. Laffey (2003), p. 83.
15. *Mayo News* (26 January 1907).
16. *Ibid.*
17. Gildea (1936), p. 141.
18. Laffey (2003), pp. 84–5.
19. Joyce (1992), pp. 22, 24.
20. Beattie (2010), p. 125.
21. *Western People* (13 January 1894).
22. *Mayo News* (23 October 1996).
23. Interview with Eithne Brogan (20 March 2014).
24. *Ibid.*
25. Ferriter, D., *A Nation of Extremes: The Pioneers in Twentieth-Century Ireland* (Dublin, 2008), p. 72.
26. *Ibid.*
27. Interview with Michael Stanton (21 November 2013).
28. *Ibid.*
29. *Ibid.*
30. Laffey, J., *Labourers in the Vineyard: The Religious of Foxford and Its Hinterland* (Foxford, 2012), p. xi.
31. *Ibid.*, pp. 28–30.
32. *Ibid.*, pp. 182–3.
33. *Ibid.*, pp. 201–4.

Chapter 10 – Later Years

1. FÁS Heritage Project, vol. 2 (Foxford, 1996), p. 128.
2. Laffey (2012), p. 161.
3. Interview with Emma Sherry (20 March 2014).

4. Interview with Bernadette Kimmerling (8 August 2012).
5. *Western People* (30 April 1932).
6. McDonagh (1994), pp. 87–8.
7. *Western People* (8 August 1936).
8. www.archive.thetablet.co.uk/article/5th-december-1936/26/a-nun-in-business (accessed 14 January 2014).
9. *Ibid.*
10. Mrs W. M. O'Brien, 'Mother Arsenius of Foxford by Fr Denis Gildea' in *The Irish Monthly*, vol. 64 (760) (Irish Jesuit Province, 1936), p. 710.
11. Depuis (2009), p. 184.
12. *Western People* (3 June 1933).
13. Beattie (2010), p. 29.
14. Interview with Margaret Maloney (28 November 2013).
15. *Ibid.*
16. *Ibid.*
17. Interview with Emma Sherry (20 March 2014).
18. Interview with Imelda Turnbull (25 January 2014).
19. Interview with Canon Michael Joyce (21 November 2013).
20. Memoirs of Agnes Morrogh-Bernard, 7 April 1921 (copy, Foxford, unpublished).
21. *Ibid.*
22. Interview with Imelda Turnbull (25 January 2014).
23. Quigley (1983), p. 54.
24. *Ibid.*
25. *The Ballina Herald* (29 January 1949).
26. Gildea (1936), p. 196.
27. *Western People Heritage Day Extra* (11 July 2007).
28. *Ibid.*
29. Ryan, J., 'A Centenary and a Golden Jubilee: Mother Morrogh-Bernard and the Providence Woollen Mills 1892–1842', in *An Irish Quarterly Review* (1942), vol. 3, no. 122, pp. 229–36.
30. *Ibid.*, p. 236.
31. *Irish Press* (12 September 1936).
32. *The Connacht Sentinel* (10 September 1963).
33. *The Connaught Telegraph* (10 April 1985).
34. Interview with Frankie Devaney (14 November 2013).
35. *The Sunday Business Post* (15 June 2008).
36. Laffey (2012), p. 384.
37. Interview with Ivars Zauers (7 May 2014).
38. *Ibid.*
39. Laffey (2012), p. 385.
40. Interview with Joe Queenan (7 October 2013).

41. *Mayo News* (1 November 1988).
42. *The Sunday Business Post* (15 June 2008).
43. Interview with Joe Queenan (7 October 2013).
44. *Ibid.*
45. *Ibid.*
46. Interview with Margaret Maloney (28 November 2013).
47. *Western People* (6 September 1995).
48. Interview with Margaret Maloney (28 November 2013).
49. Interview with Frankie Devaney (14 November 2013).
50. Interview with Peter Hynes (1 May 2014).
51. Burke, E., 'Foxford Woollen Mills Visitor Centre', in *Mayo Association, Dublin, 1993 Yearbook* (Dublin, 1993), p. 75.
52. *Mayo News* (14 February 1996).
53. *Western People* (16 April 1996).
54. *Mayo News* (16 June 1993).
55. *Ibid.*
56. Interview with Eithne Brogan (20 March 2014).
57. Interview with Margaret Maloney (28 November 2013).
58. Clear (1987), p. xix.
59. *Ibid.*
60. Dublin Hospitals Commission, *Report of the Commission of Inquiry into the Management and Working of Dublin Hospitals Together with Minutes of Evidence and Appendices 1887 C 5042 XXXV.1* (Great Britain Parliament) (Dublin, 1887), p. 134.
61. Luddy, M., 'Philanthropy in Nineteenth-Century Ireland', in *The Field Day Anthology of Irish Writing*, vol. v (Cork, 2002), pp. 691–2, 694, 703.
62. McDonagh (1994), p. 97.
63. Butler, H., *The Eggman and the Fairies: Irish Essays*, edited by J. Banville (London, 2012), p. 204.
64. Gildea (1936), p. 198.
65. Interview with Imelda Turnbull (25 January 2014).

Bibliography

Aguinis, M., *Admiral William Brown: Liberator of the South Atlantic* (The Admiral Brown Society, Foxford, 2006)

Ardagh, J., *Ireland and the Irish: Portrait of a Changing Society* (Hamish Hamilton, London, 1994)

Bardon, J., *A History of Ireland in 250 Episodes* (Gill & Macmillan, Dublin, 2008)

Beattie, J., *Foxford Folklore – Changing Times: The 1938 Schools Collection Revisited* (Foxford Rural Social Scheme, Foxford, 2010)

Beuner, C. S., 'Coping with Want in the West: A Permanent Local Remedy, What An Irish Nun Has Done', in *New Zealand Tablet*, vol. xxvi (15 July 1898)

Bielenberg, A. and Breathnach, C., *Family income and expenditure in the West of Ireland: the evidence from the Baseline Reports of the Congested Districts Board* (*Historical National Accounts Group for Ireland*, Cork, 2000)

Biggs-Davison, J., *George Wyndham: A Study in Toryism* (Hodder & Stoughton, London, 1951)

Bingham-Daly, T., *The Mayo Binghams* (The Pentland Press, Bishop Auckland, 1997)

Birmingham, G. A., *Hyacinth* (Hodder & Stoughton, London, 1906)

Breathnach, C., *The Congested Districts Board of Ireland 1891–1923* (Four Courts Press, Dublin, 2005)

Browne, N., *Against the Tide* (Gill & Macmillan, Dublin, 1986)

Bull, P., *Land, Politics, and Nationalism: A Study of the Irish Land Question* (Gill & Macmillan, Dublin, 1996)

Burke, E., 'Foxford Woollen Mills Visitor Centre', in *Mayo Association, Dublin, 1993 Yearbook* (Avelbury Ltd, Dublin, 1993)

Butler, H., *The Eggman and the Faries: Irish Essays*, edited by J. Banville (Notting Hill Editions, London, 2012)

Butler, M. M., *A Candle Was Lit: The Life of Mother Mary Aikenhead* (Cloonmore & Reynolds, Dublin, 1953)

Campbell, F., *Nationalist Politics in the West of Ireland 1891–1892* (Oxford University Press, New York, 2005)

Campbell Gordon Aberdeen, J., and Gordon Aberdeen, I., *We Twa: Reminiscences of Lord and Lady Aberdeen*, vol. i (London, W. Collins, Sons & Co., London, 1925)

Clancy, P., *A Journey of Mercy from Birth to Re-Birth* (Congregation of the Sisters of Mercy, Mayo, 1994)

Clarke, F., 'Agnes Morrogh-Bernard (Mother Mary Arsenius)', in Quinn, J. and McGuire J. (eds) *Dictionary of Irish Biography* (Cambridge University Press, Cambridge, 2009)

Clear, C., *Nuns in Nineteenth-Century Ireland* (Gill & Macmillan, Dublin, 1987)

Collins, M., *The Path to Freedom* (Mercier Press, Cork, 1995)

Comerford, V., 'Gladstone's First Irish Enterprise 1864–1870', in Vaughan, W. E. and Moody, T. W. (eds), *A New History of Ireland: Ireland under the Union 1801–1870* (Clarendon Press, Oxford, 1989)

Coogan, T. P., *The Famine Plot: England's Role in Ireland's Greatest Tragedy* (Palgrave Macmillan, New York, 2012)

Cooke, C., *Mary Charles Walker: The Nun of Calabar* (Four Courts Press, Dublin, 1980)

Coolahan, J., 'The Development of Educational Studies and Teacher Education', in *Ireland in Education Research and Perspectives* (NUI, Maynooth, 2004)

Crowley, J. *et al.*, *Atlas of the Great Irish Famine 1845–52* (Cork University Press, Cork, 2012)

Cruise-O'Brien, M., *The Same Age As The State* (The O'Brien Press, Dublin, 2003)

Curtis, L. P., *The Depiction of Eviction In Ireland 1845–1910* (UCD Press, Dublin, 2011)

Curtis, L. P., *Coercion and Conciliation in Ireland: A study in Conservative Unionism* (Princeton Book Co., New Jersey, 1963)

Daly, M. E., *The First Department: A History of the Department of Agriculture* (Institute of Public Administration, Dublin, 2002)

Davitt, M., *The Fall of Feudalism in Ireland* (Harper & Brothers, London, 1904)

Davitt, M., *Jottings in Solitary*, edited by C. King (UCD Press, Dublin, 2003)

Depuis, N., *Mná Na hÉireann: Women Who Shaped Ireland* (Mercier Press, Cork, 2009)

Dooley, T., *The Land for the People: The Land Question in Independent Ireland* (UCD Press, Dublin, 2004)

Dooley, T., *The Big Houses and Landed Estates of Ireland: A Research Guide* (Four Courts Press, Dublin, 2007)

Dun, F., *Landlords and Tenants in Ireland* (Longmans Green & Co., Dublin, 1881)

Dunleavy, J., 'Keir Hardie's Visit to Mayo in 1906', in *JWHS*, vol. 10 (Westport Historical Society, Westport, 1990)

Ferriter, D., *A Nation of Extremes: The Pioneers in Twentieth-Century Ireland* (Irish Academic Press, Dublin, 2008)

Ferriter, D., *The Transformation of Ireland 1900–2000* (Profile Books, London, 2004)

Finlay, T. A., 'Foxford Then and Now', in *New Ireland Review*, vol. xiv (Dublin, 1900)

Finlay, T. A., *Foxford and the Providence Woollen Mills* (Fallon & Co., Dublin, 1940)

Forristal, D., *The Second Burial of Bishop Shanahan* (Veritas, Dublin, 1990)

Fry, E., *James Hack Tuke: A Memoir* (Macmillan, London, 1899)

Gatty, C. T., *Recognita* (John Murray, London, 1917)

Gildea, D., *Mother Mary Arsenius of Foxford* (Burns Oates & Washbourne Ltd, Dublin, 1936)

Greer, J., *The Windings of the Moy* (Alex Thom & Co. Ltd, Dublin, 1924)

Gregory, A. and Paseta, S., *Ireland and the Great War: A War to Unite Us All* (Manchester University Press, Manchester, 2002)

Gribbon, H. D., 'Economic and Social History 1850–1921' in Vaughan, W. E. and Moody, T. W. (eds), *A New History of Ireland: Ireland under the Union 1870–1921* (Oxford University Press, Oxford, 1996)

Hackett, R., *Religion in Calabar: The Religious Life and History of a Nigerian Town* (Mouton de Gruyter, Berlin, 1988)

Hayes, A. and Urquart, D., *The Irish Women's History Reader* (Routledge, London, 2001)

Heaney M. J., *Galway and Mayo Families* (unpublished, Castlebar, *c.* 1984)

Helland, J., 'A Delightful Change of Fashion: Fair trade, Cottage Craft, and Tweed in Late Nineteenth-Century Ireland', in *The Canadian Journal of Irish Studies*, vol. 36, no. 2 (2010).

Henry, C., 'The Swinford Union Poor Law Administration', in Garavin, J., *The Mayo Association Year Book 1998* (Mayo Association, Dublin, 1997)

Hickey, D. J. and Doherty, J. E., *A Dictionary of Irish History 1800–1980* (Gill & Macmillan, Dublin, 1980)

Hinkson, P., *Seventy Years Young: Memories of Elizabeth Countess of Fingall* (The Lilliput Press, Dublin, 1991)

Hospitals Commission, *Report of the Commission of Inquiry into the Management and Working of Dublin Hospitals Together with Minutes of Evidence and Appendices 1887* C 5042 XXXV.1 (Great Britain, Parliament) (H.M. Stationery Office, Dublin 1887)

Jordan, D. E., *Land and Popular Politics in Ireland: County Mayo from the Plantation to the Land War* (Cambridge University Press, Cambridge 1994)

Joyce, B., *Agnes Morrogh-Bernard 1842–1932: Foundress of the Foxford Woollen Mills* (Foxford IRD, Foxford, 1992)

Keane, M., *Ishbel: Lady Aberdeen in Ireland* (Colour Point Books, Newtownards, 1999)

Kernaghan, P., *Watching for Daybreak: A History of St Matthew's Parish, Belfast* (St Matthew's Parish, Belfast, 2000)

Kinealy, C., *This Great Calamity: The Irish Famine 1845–52* (Gill & Macmillan, Dublin, 1994)

King, C., 'The Recess Committee 1895–96', in *Studia Hibernica*, no. 30 (St Patrick's College, Dublin, 1998/99)

King, C. *et al.*, *The West of Ireland: New Perspectives on the Nineteenth Century* (The History Press Ireland, Dublin, 2011)

Kissane, B., *The Politics of the Irish Civil War* (Oxford University Press, Oxford, 2005)

Laffey, J., *Foxford Through the Arches of Time* (Foxford Book Committee, Foxford, 2003)

Laffey, J., *Labourers in the Vineyard: The Religious of Foxford and Its Hinterland* (Foxford Book Committee, Foxford, 2012)

Lee, J., *The Modernisation of Irish Society 1848–1918* (Clarendon Press, Dublin, 1973)

Leen, E., 'A Great Irish Missionary: Bishop Joseph Shanahan CSSp.', in *Studies*, vol. 33 (June 1944)

Lenihan, P., *Consolidating Conquest Ireland 1603-1727* (Pearson Education, Harlow, 2008)

Luddy, M., 'Philanthropy in Nineteenth-Century Ireland', in *The Field Day Anthology of Irish Writing*, vol. v (Cork University Press, Cork, 2002)

Lysaght, C., *Great Irish Lives* (Harper Collins, London, 2008)

Bibliography

Madden, F. J., *Teach Yourself The History of Ireland* (Hodder Education, London, 2005)

Magray Peckham, M., *The Transforming Power of the Nuns: Women, Religious, and Cultural Change in Ireland 1750–1900* (Oxford University Press, New York, 1998)

Maguire, C., 'The Health of the Irish People', in *Studies*, vol. 5 (Dublin, 1913)

Manning, M., *James Dillon: A Biography* (Wolfhound Press, Dublin, 1999)

Masahiko, Y., 'George A. Bermingham. *General John Regan*: A Hearty Wish for Reconciliation Between Every Human Being', in *JWHS*, vol. 30 (Westport Historical Society, Westport, 2012)

Matthews, P. J., *Revival: The Abbey Theatre, Sinn Féin, the Gaelic League and the Co-operative Movement* (Cork University in association with Field Day, Cork, 2003)

Maume, P., *The Long Gestation: Irish Nationalist Life 1891–1918* (Gill & Macmillan, Dublin, 1999)

McCaffrey, C., *In Search of Ireland's Heroes* (Ivan R. Dee, Chicago, 2006)

McCarthy-Filgate, W. T. M., *Irish Rural Life and Industry with Suggestions for the Future* (Hely's Ltd, Dublin, 1907)

McDonagh, E. (ed.), *Survival or Salvation: A Second Mayo Book of Theology* (The Columba Press, Dublin, 1994)

McDonagh, M., *The Life of William O'Brien: The Irish Nationalist* (Ernest Benn Ltd, London, 1928)

McDonnell-Garvey, M., *The Ancient Territory of Sliabh Lugha Mid-Connacht* (Drumlin Publications, Manorhamilton, 1995)

McGill, J., 'The Irish Woollen Industry from Earliest to Donegal Homespuns', in *Journal of the Donegal Historical Society* (Donegal Historical Society, 1949)

McPherson, D. A., *Women and the Irish Nation: Gender, Culture and Irish Identity 1890–1914* (Palgrave Macmillan, New York, 2012)

Meehan, R., *The Story of Mayo* (Mayo County Council, Castlebar, 2003)

Micks, W. L., *An Account of the Congested Districts Board for Ireland 1891–1923* (Eason & Son, Dublin, 1925)

Miller, K., *Emigrants and Exiles: Ireland and Her Irish Exodus to North America* (Oxford University Press, New York, 1985)

Mitchell, G., *Deeds not Words: The Life and Work of Muriel Gahan* (Townhouse, Dublin, 1997)

Mokyr, J., *Why Ireland Starved: A Quantitative and Analytical History of the Irish Economy, 1800–1850* (Allen & Unwin, London, 1985)

Murray, P., 'Novels, Nuns and the Revival of Irish Industries: The Rector of Westport and the Foxford Woollen Mill 1905–1907', in *JWHS*, vol. 8 (Westport Historical Society, Westport, 1988)

Nelson, B. *Irish Nationalists and the Making of the Irish Race* (Princeton University Press, Princeton, 2012)

Nolan, R., *Within the Mullet* (Standard Printing, Galway, 2000)

Ó Broin, L., *The Chief Secretary: Augustine Birrell in Ireland* (Chatto & Windus, London, 1969)

O'Grada, C., *A New Economic History 1780–1939* (Oxford University Press, New York, 1995)

O'Grada, C., *Ireland's Great Famine: Interdisciplinary Perspectives* (UCD Press, Dublin, 2006)

O'Hara, B., *Davitt* (Mayo County Council, Castlebar, 2006)

O'Riordan, M., *Catholicity and Progress in Ireland* (Kegan Paul, Trench, Trübner & Co. Ltd, London, 1906)

O'Sullivan, M., *Mary Robinson: The Life and Times of an Irish Liberal* (Blackwater Press, Dublin, 1993)

Pentland, M., *A Bonnie Fechter* (Batsford, London, 1952)

Preston, W., 'Life and Writings of William Preston 1753–1807', in *Studies* (Dublin, 1942)

Purdon, E., *The Irish Civil War 1922–1923* (Mercier Press, Cork, 2000)

Quigley, A. A., *Green Is My Sky* (Avoca Publications, Dublin, 1983)

Reid, T., *Travels in Ireland in the Year 1822: Exhibiting Brief Sketches of the Moral, Physical, and Political State of the Country: with Reflections on the Best Means of Improving Its Condition* (Longman & Hurst, London, 1823)

Richards, S., 'Ireland Real and Ideal', in *The Cambridge Companion to Twentieth-Century Irish Drama* (Cambridge University Press, Cambridge, 2004)

Ryan, J., 'A Centenary and a Golden Jubilee: Mother Morrogh-Bernard and the Providence Woollen Mills 1892–1842', in *An Irish Quarterly Review* (Irish Province of the Society of Jesus, Dublin, 1942)

Shannon, C. B., *Arthur J. Balfour and Ireland 1874–1922* (The Catholic University of America Press, Washington, 1988)

Smyth, I., 'A Dream to Follow', in *Healing and Development Yearbook 2001* (Rosemount Publications, Dublin, 2001)

Sullivan, M., *Mary Robinson: The Life and Times of an Irish Liberal* (Blackwater Press, Dublin, 1993)

Swords, L., *In Their Own Words: The Famine in North Connacht 1845–1849* (The Columba Press, Dublin, 1999)

Swords, L., *A Dominant Church: The Diocese of Achonry 1818–1960* (The Columba Press, Dublin, 2004)

The Irish Tourist Association Topographical and General Survey (Irish Tourist Association, Dublin, 1945)

Travers, P., *Settlements and Divisions Ireland 1870–1922* (Hellicon Ltd, Dublin, 1988)

Tuke, J. H., *Irish Distress and Its Remedies: A Visit to Donegal and Connaught, February, March and April 1880* (Ridgeway, Michigan, 1880)

Tuke, J. H., *Ought Emigration from Ireland to be Assisted?* (A. Strahan, London, 1882)

West, T., *Horace Plunkett: Co-operation and Politics: An Irish Biography* (Colin Smythe Ltd, Gerrard's Cross, 1986)

Williams, W. H. A., *Landscape, Tourism, and the Irish Character: British Travel Writers in Pre-Famine Ireland 1750–1850* (The University of Wisconsin Press, Wisconsin, 2008)

Woodham-Smith, C., *The Great Hunger* (Penguin Books, London, 1991)

Lightning Source UK Ltd.
Milton Keynes UK
UKHW021816220223
417460UK00012B/227